GOLF IN THE ANCIEI NORTHUMB]

A MAGICAL PLACE OF NATURAL BEAUTY, RICH HISTORY, ENGAGING SETTLEMENTS AND FINE GOLF COURSES

by

JOHN AND REBECCA ROGERS

ERGO PRESS
Publishing for Northumberland

GOLF IN THE ANCIENT KINGDOM
OF NORTHUMBERLAND

Published by ERGO PRESS 2008

Photographs by the authors and Alan I Grint.

Cover graphics by Slim Palmer

www.slimpalmer.com

ISBN: 978-0-9557510-1-1

Front Cover: Bamburgh Castle from Bamburgh Castle Golf Course
Back Cover: Golf Course at De Vere Slaley Hall

ERGO PRESS
5, St Mary's Chare
Hexham
Northumberland
NE46 1NQ
00 44 (0)1434 689653
www.ergopress.com
ergo.press@yahoo.co.uk

CONTENTS

FOREWORD

HIS GRACE, THE DUKE OF NORTHUMBERLAND

As Northumberland's worst golfer, I am the least likely candidate to write a foreword for a book about golf. I have occasionally sliced a ball around the course at Foxton (which, incidentally, is ideally laid out for the right handed 'slicer' as the ball curls away from the cliffs above the cold North Sea), but I cannot claim any passion for the game. For me, the joy of any sport is playing in beautiful surroundings, and few places are as beautiful as Northumberland.

This book takes the golfer beyond the game, to a land rich in the diversity of its landscape, history and culture, where early Christianity and centuries of border warfare shaped its early architectural heritage as much as agricultural and industrial revolutions shaped its more recent history. It is a land of heroes and villains, of castles and abbeys, long, sandy beaches, heather clad hills and sparkling rivers – and amongst all this lie wonderful golf courses!

I am sure that anyone interested in the region will be fascinated by this well-researched and extremely interesting book. I am equally sure that for a golfer, it will add a new dimension to the game.

AUTHORS' INTRODUCTION

This book is about golf courses. But it's also about Northumberland, one of the most consistently beautiful of all English counties. The first are the jewels, the second the crown in which they are set.

It was not golf that first brought us to Northumberland. It was a desire to escape the congestion that dogged us while touring in England's south in 1998. There was a limit to our tolerance of long queues, no matter how fine the attractions at their end, or of the life-threatening crush of tourist buses on the roads, no matter how attractive the surrounding scenery. After a couple of weeks we longed for the space and ease of movement we took for granted in Australia, but with the scenery and history that motivated our holiday in the first place. Coincidentally we happened upon a reference in a touring guide to Northumberland, not a place we had ever considered, or for that matter heard much about. The guide described the county as "England's last great wilderness – an empty and unspoilt corner of England with wonderful scenery", so off we went. We found everything that we had hoped for: history, scenery and plenty of space, concluding that we had stumbled on one of England's best kept secrets.

Such was Northumberland's impact on us during that holiday that six months later we returned and bought a cottage in Alnwick, determined that it was to be our second home. We have never had reason either to doubt our decision, or to find a better place to live in Britain. Being keen golfers, we soon sought out the local courses; after playing a number of these that we realised that the secret we were sharing extended to more than the beauty of Northumberland: it included some of the finest, least expensive, accessible and welcoming courses in Britain. We hadn't considered golf in our decision to spend part of our year in Northumberland, but we have since come to appreciate this unexpected bonus.

Surprisingly, the county is largely ignored in the literature on golf in Britain. Surely, we thought, it deserves better recognition, given that it has superb seaside links courses and, if one tires of the wind, seascape and rugged terrain, other courses inland presenting different vistas and challenges. This led naturally to our decision to write a book on our discovery of what we describe as the four 'virtues' of Northumberland: its scenery, its rich history, its settlements and places and its wonderful golf courses. Any one of these alone might warrant a visit from the golfing tourist, but the four combined makes the place simply irresistible. We hope our book encourages more visitors to visit Northumberland, and we promise them one thing without fear of reproach: they will not be disappointed in what they find, whether or not they are golfers. It is truly a magical place.

ACKNOWLEDGEMENTS

Completion of this project owes much to the help and support given to us by our many Northumbrian friends. Of these we must give special thanks to John and Marjorie Chilton. They have been the most loyal of mates, but more than this they have stimulated our interest in the history and geography of Northumberland, kept us supplied with relevant books and other research material, answered our barrage of questions with scholarship and patience, played hundreds of rounds of golf with us and treated us as family. We can say without hesitation that there is a good chance that without their inspiration and help this book may not have been started, let alone finished. Also, Adrian and Elizabeth Herd and Mark and Sylvia Anderson have given us wonderful company and hospitality over the years. Their friendship has sustained and enriched us. Our friends are entitled to share in anything that is worthy in the book, but they cannot be blamed for anything that is not.

THE VIRTUE OF SPACE AND BEAUTY

Northumberland can rightly claim a number of distinctions. For example, it boasts, among other things, that it's the only English county to have its own flag and tartan, that it has more castles open to the public than any other county, that it contains the largest world heritage site (Hadrian's Wall), that it has its own musical instrument (the Northumbrian pipes), and that it even has its own anthem. The Northumbrian dialect is like no other.

But a far more obvious – and affecting – distinction is the wonderful sense of space and accessibility in contrast with the congestion in England's south.

Northumberland is the most northerly county in England, and one of its largest and least polluted. With a total area of almost 2000 square miles, and a population of only 307,000, Northumberland is one of the least densely populated counties in England, having a population density of 158 persons per square mile, compared to the national figure of 960 per square mile. Northumberland has no cities – the largest centres are the market towns of Morpeth, Berwick-upon-Tweed, Hexham and Alnwick. Morpeth is the largest with a population of only 14,400. A little less than half the population of Northumberland lives in the urban southeast corner, in an area within commuting distance of Newcastle-upon-Tyne in the adjoining county of Tyne and Wear. This heavily populated area covers less than five per cent of the region's total land area.

So it is that most of Northumberland's roads have little traffic and are rarely without long scenic views. The towns and villages are relatively uncrowded and easy to park in. You don't wait for hours in queues to historic sites and many of the attractions are free and unfettered. You can go long distances on the many walking tracks without meeting another person, as is the case with the beaches. This relative emptiness is valuable because it offers the maximum opportunity to enjoy Northumberland's magnificent scenery.

The landscape of Northumberland is the product of a succession of great geological events. The first are the great volcanic upheavals that 400 million years ago formed the Cheviot Hills. Then followed the Carboniferous period during which, over millions of years, mud and sand were deposited into the shallow sea that covered much of Northumberland at the time, and combined under pressure with the lime of shells from marine organisms to form the sandstone and limestone that prevail as Northumberland's rocks. Sea levels rose and fell, and when the land was exposed it was colonised by lush forests and ferns which, as they decayed and were covered by mud and sand, formed the coal seams so abundant in the county's southeast corner.

This was followed by an Ice Age that began 2.5 million years ago and lasted for about 1 million years. In this era, an ice sheet from Scotland scoured the landscape, smoothed the hillsides and moved surface soil and boulders. This eroded material was deposited as boulder clay in valleys and over the coastal plain that is today's Northumberland's richest agricultural land.

One change occurring during these great events gave the county one of its most distinctive geological features: at the end of the Carboniferous period, some 200 million years ago, molten volcanic material spread horizontally to solidify between, and to push up, the bedding planes of the sedimentary rocks. This resulted in the Great Whin Sill, which underlies much of eastern and southern Northumberland and runs southwards into the Pennines and County Durham. It forms the Farne Islands and in places has given rise to bold escarpments as high as 250 feet which have been well exploited by military engineers for centuries. The Romans used sections of the Sill to site long runs of their Wall and outcrops were later used as sites for castles at Holy Island, Dunstanburgh and Bamburgh. The elevation allowed by the Sill has distinguished Northumberland's 'castles in the sky'.

Speaking very broadly, there are five main areas of natural attraction in Northumberland:

The Cheviot Hills are the result of erosion of the ancient volcanic lavas. In its centre of these hills is Cheviot, made up of granite which plugged these ancient volcanoes

Dominating the western boundary of Northumberland are the Cheviot Hills, 200 square miles of the grandest scenery to be found anywhere. The Cheviot, at 2610 feet, is the apex. Treeless and desolate, the Cheviots comprise some of the highest and wildest moorland in England. Regarded as a walkers' paradise, they offer the finest scenery imaginable – a vast expanse of grass, heather and peat with an array of plants and wildlife many of which have been lost in other areas of the country. The hills are the watershed of the many fast rivers flowing through steep-sided wooded valleys to the North Sea.

Including and extending east of the Cheviots is one of the last great open spaces in Britain – the Northumberland National Park. This occupies high country of between 600 to 1000 feet running from The Cheviot to the River Tyne in the south. Covering some 400 square miles, the Park offers a vast variety of landscapes including mountains, moorland, high hills, wooded valleys and large areas of forest.

Contiguous with, and to the southwest of, the National Park, is the Border Forest Park, which at 230 square miles is Britain's largest man-made forest (predominantly of spruce and pine varieties). It has hills, rivers and open spaces, and a vast array of wildlife including red squirrels and three species of deer. At its heart is Kielder Water, the largest man-made lake in Western Europe with a shoreline of 27 miles. The lake is the main reason why there is never a water shortage in Northumberland even though the county is one of the driest in Britain – another plus for visitors.

Together these three areas – the Cheviot Hills, National Park and Border Forest Park – constitute a band of country of exceptional natural beauty covering nearly half of Northumberland's total territory. It occupies the western side of the county from the Scottish border to Hadrian's Wall in the south with the Cheviot Hills forming the county's backbone along the border with Cumbria.

To the south, in Northumberland's western corner bounded on two sides by Cumbria and Durham, is the region of the North Pennines covering some 1000 square acres, the most northern reach of the great Pennines chain. The North Pennines is a region of magnificent moorland, valleys, waterfalls and streams and wonderful wildlife, and has been formally declared an Area of Outstanding Natural Beauty. It is more gently contoured than the Cheviot Hills, being formed by sedimentary action and thus not subjected to the latter's violent volcanic convulsions and glacial reconstruction.

Separating the Cheviot Hills to the north and the North Pennines to the south is the Tyne Valley, a band of gentle pastoral land running west-east along either side of the South Tyne and Tyne rivers (the last formed by the union at Hexham of the South and North Tynes). The South Tyne rises in the Pennines on the bleak Alston Moor and the North Tyne in the Border Forest area of the Cheviots. Hadrian's Wall runs along the northern edge of the valley atop the Whin Sill.

The Whin Sill runs all the way through Northern England including Cumbria and Durham. In the south of Northumberland it forms steep escarpments along which Hadrian's Wall extends; in the north it forms sea cliffs, islands and the hills on which castles were built.

The coastline – the lordly strand of Northumberland – is reason alone to visit the county. Declared both an Area of Outstanding Natural Beauty and a Heritage Coast, the strand stretches 40 miles from Amble northwards to the Scottish border. Along it are found rocky cliffs, sand dunes, long stretches of empty beaches of fine white sand, quaint fishing villages, broad estuaries, the aptly named Holy Island and the wildlife sanctuary of the

Farne Islands. Well protected from development, there is little along the coastline to mar its beauty. It can be said without hesitation that the coast of Northumberland need not fear comparison with many of the famous coastal strips around the world that grace tourist brochures. Indeed, they often hold surf carnivals along this coast. But the coast is not only an important asset for beach goers and sightseers; golfers too benefit when playing the county's seaside courses that hug the coast and offer wonderful seascapes.

Finally, there is the pastoral land on the coastal plain stretching in a north-south band from the Scottish border to Newcastle. This plain is at its widest between Newcastle and Morpeth while at its centre, south of Alnwick, it's reduced to a narrow strip a little more than a mile wide. Northumberland is above all an agricultural county, one of the more productive farming areas of Britain. This fact will come as no surprise to visitors who can't escape the engaging sight of professionally tended farms punctuated by woodlands and defined by hedgerows. The farmland panorama is most noticeable from high vantage points and even offers compensation for the drive through Northumberland along the narrow and often slow A1.

The scenery on offer commends itself particularly to walkers who can, with ease, find well-marked and well-mapped walks of all types and degrees of difficulty. These can be in the Cheviots, on moorland, along river valleys, across rich farmland and along stretches of beaches and dunes. More often that not you will be alone to enjoy the scenery without distraction. Of course if walking isn't your thing, much of the beauty is easily enjoyed from a car.

Northumberland is an oasis of beauty, tranquility and space and long may this blissful state continue. This assessment was validated in October 2006 when the Campaign to Protect Rural England identified Northumberland as the "most tranquil" of all England's counties.

THE VIRTUE OF RICH AND RARE HISTORY

Hhistory was not the reason for us visiting Northumberland – after all there is no shortage of places of historical interest in Britain – but it is an important reason for our attachment to the place. We sensed after a short time here that there was something rich and rare about Northumberland's past and we set out to discover what this was. This chapter tries to explain what we discovered and to give some context to the places and sites, and to the golf courses that the golfing tourist might visit.

We shall skip over the very ancient days of the county's human settlement, dating from 6000BC, and pick up our story where the written historical record begins – with Roman settlement.

ROMAN SETTLEMENT

The Romans arrived in the land that is now Northumberland in 71AD and established a base in the Tyne Valley. Here they built a line of forts along the River Tyne and a network of roads to supply them. By 81AD they had expanded their control to the narrow neck of land between the Firth of Forth and the River Clyde along which they build another line of forts. The two lines of forts were joined by a north-south military road known now as Dere Street which was protected by a series of camps, one of which, Chew Green, we discuss later.

In 122AD the Emperor Hadrian visited Britain and ordered the construction of a stone wall from Newcastle to the Solway Firth. This 'Hadrian's Wall' followed closely the lateral line of forts along the River Tyne. Thus was built the finest Roman monument in Britain – we return to it later.

The Celtic tribe occupying the land to the east of the Cheviots between the Scottish border and Hadrian's Wall was called the *Votadini*. The *Votadini* were principally farmers, and were a deeply superstitious people with an organized religion and priesthood (Druids). They had a formidable military class operating from strong hilltop fortifications such as Traprain Law in southern Scotland and Yeavering Bell outside Wooler. Presumably the Romans at first had a hard time suppressing the locals, but by 221AD the *Votadini* and the Romans were fighting together, uniting against the raiding Picts (Roman *Picti* – 'painted people'). The *Votadini* maintained their independence under their kings and were regarded as 'loyal' by the Romans.

Building the Wall
by William Bell Scott,
a tapestry painting
which can be seen at
Wallington Hall,
near Morpeth

As a result of this alliance, the *Votadini* learned Roman military discipline and tactics; they were also instructed in horsemanship by the mercenaries brought by the Romans from their provinces in Germanic Europe. There is evidence that Roman officers were attached to *Votadini* forces to develop their military capability.

This capability was to prove important, for in 383AD the Romans, under sustained attack from the Picts and other hostile peoples, were forced to abandon Hadrian's Wall, and in 410AD withdrew their legions from Britain to defend their continental empire from Barbarian attack. The British were on their own.

THE BRITISH HEROIC AGE

What had been the *Votadini* homeland was divided into two kingdoms. One was in southern Scotland, centred on Edinburgh; the other, Bryneich, was in the land between the Tweed and Tyne and was ruled principally from Yeavering Bell; this roughly coincided with the territory of modern Northumberland.

In the 200 years after the Roman withdrawal, the battle-hardened northern tribes defended their land, first against the Picts and later against the Germanic Anglo-Saxons. It was what historian Peter Blair styles (in *Northumbria in the Days of Bede)* the "British Heroic Age".

The Anglo-Saxons, who were later to refer to themselves as *Englisc*, had settled around the Humber's tidal estuary before spreading west and north along river valleys. From this process of gradual settlement emerged the territorial entity known as Deira, embracing land from the Humber to the River Tyne with York as its nucleus. This became the first homeland of the Anglo-Saxon occupiers and the bridgehead for their spread northwards.

In 547AD, the Anglo-Saxons came from Deira by sea and seized Bamburgh. Thereafter, for a period of around fifty years, the Anglo-Saxons met fierce resistance from the British who were able to restrict their advance, but who, finally exhausted from fighting on two fronts, were defeated by the Germans in a major victory at Catterick, thereby finally ending British resistance. It's at this point that Bryneich became known as Bernicia from the Anglo-Saxon pronunciation *Beornicce*.

By 604AD the two English kingdoms of Bernicia and Deria were united as the kingdom of *Northanhymbre* which in the succeeding decade brought much of northern England and Wales under its sway. The kingdom was later expanded to include what are modern day Leeds, Anglesey and the Isle of Man.

The Northumberland of the 7th and 8th Centuries had a formidable military capacity and used it often in battles with other kingdoms. This power was most manifest in the period between 617AD and 685AD, when four of Northumberland's kings were accorded the rank of ruler, or high king (*Bretenanwealda*) of Britain. However, the kingdom suffered a setback in 685AD when it suffered a defeat in a campaign against the Picts and thereafter its authority over the Picts and Scots crumbled for ever. Historians see this point as marking the decline of Northumbrian military power leading to a contraction of its colonized territory.

But while its military power waned, Northumberland's Christian influence soared.

This began in 627AD when the king, Edwin, converted to Christianity in a ceremony in which 3000 of his subjects were also baptized on the banks of the River Glen in the shadow of Yeavering Bell. In the mid 7th Century, Edwin's successor bought Aidan, later Saint Aidan, an eminent ecclesiastic, from Iona to assist the further conversion of his people from a monastery on Lindisfarne (Holy Island).

From this humble beginning, Northumberland was to develop into an influential centre of Christianity in Anglo-Saxon England, remarkable for its missionaries, scholarship and art, the influence of which extended well beyond the borders of the kingdom. Churchmen, builders and artists from

Northumberland influenced the conversion and cultural development of Scotland and the English Midlands, and rulers of mainland Europe sent for books and clergy to help reform their churches. Lindisfarne was at the heart of this religious movement, with a number of exceptional monastic superiors, five of whom were made saints.

One of these warrants particular mention. Some time around 663AD, Cuthbert, the Prior of Melrose, was brought to Lindisfarne to be its Prior. He spent little time there however, preferring an ascetic life on one of the Farne Islands. In around 685AD Cuthbert was appointed Bishop of Lindisfarne. He was associated with a number of miracles, and it's claimed that when his body was exhumed 11 years after his death in 687, it was entirely uncorrupted. Naturally, he was canonised.

The veneration of Cuthbert led to the production in 721AD of one of the truly great works of Northumbrian religious art, the *Lindisfarne Gospels*. This magnificent book of the four Gospels was written on 258 pages of the finest vellum (calfskin) and was decorated with sumptuous calligraphy and painting by a team of scribes. The *Lindisfarne Gospels* are but one example of the strength of monastic learning that flourished in the 8th Century, helped in large part by a succession of kings who managed to maintain the territory, cohesion, peace and prosperity of the kingdom.

However, this 'Golden Age' would not survive the 8th Century.

THE DANISH PERIOD

The architects of Northumberland's demise were seafaring warriors from Scandinavia, described as Northmen or Danes. Norman Davies (*The Isles: A History*) explains that the latter was a name derived from the Old English word *thegn*, used to describe a class of professional fighters. The word was adopted by the Northmen to describe territory they controlled, thus 'Danmark' (Denmark).

In 793AD the Danes attacked Lindisfarne and destroyed its monastery. This was the first of a wave of raids that destabilized the kingdom and caused the Lindisfarne monks to flee the Island, taking with them the *Lindisfarne Gospels*, the coffin of St Cuthbert and other treasures. Years later the coffin finally came to rest where Durham Cathedral came to be built, where it remains today. The original of the *Lindisfarne Gospels* is housed in the British Museum.

The raiders turned invaders and the kingdom of Northumberland was split into its two historic parts – Deira and Bernicia. From this point it is appropriate to refer to Bernicia as Northumberland and Deira as the Kingdom of York (*Jorvik*).

The nature and extent of Danish rule in the North differed in the two places. Northumberland was not heavily settled by the Danes except for a stronghold at Tynemouth. However, it was ruled first by kings and, after 954AD, by earls of Danish blood. It remained predominantly Anglo-Saxon in custom and language. On the other hand, the Kingdom of York became a Danish homeland and the base for the Danish invasion southward and westward into England.

Despite being left largely to its own devices, Northumberland was in for an awful time. While Christianity was not extinguished, the great Northumbrian monasteries, the centres of literary, artistic and spiritual life, were plundered and destroyed. Northumberland was never again to be a centre of spiritual authority and learning.

This cultural loss was accompanied by territorial loss. Throughout the 10th Century, the Scots, by a combination of military successes and concessions won from English kings eager for a Scottish alliance against the Danes, were able to acquire all of Northumberland's's territory north of the Tweed, thereby giving Scotland its border with England and its future administrative and economic base. Further attempts by the Scots to seize land south of the Tweed in the late 10th Century were beaten back; however, their territorial ambitions were undiminished.

Thus it was that Northumberland, once a powerful, independent and culturally pervasive kingdom, was conquered, humiliated and stripped of land that had been hard won and held by successive Northumbrian kings. It ceased to be viable as an independent country and was doomed to spend the next six centuries as a miserable bone over which England and Scotland fought, and on which both chewed. It could have been a different story if it had not been for the Danes; perhaps the capital of England would today be Newcastle-upon-Tyne.

THE NORMANS

After some 30 years of local resistance, the Normans (originally Danes, known to the French as *Nor Men* who settled in the Seine Valley in the late 9th Century) finally succeeded in imposing a new and entirely Norman regime on the hapless Northumbrians, by transplanting Norman barons and bishops supported by a network of castles and other fortifications (such as the 'New Castle' on the Tyne) as part of the feudal system

Nineteenth Century
etching of the ruins
of Tynemouth Priory

William the Conqueror imposed throughout England. This brought an end to 400 years of independence and semi-independence during which Northumberland, and before it Bernicia, had been ruled by 42 kings and 8 earls. During this period were built, or rebuilt, the great monasteries of Northumberland including Lindisfarne, Tynemouth, Hexham and Alnwick.

THE BLOODY SCOTS

It was less than a century after Britain's new Norman management had brought the locals to heel that Scotland staked its claim to Northumberland; this it continued to do for the next 500 years.

In 1138 Scotland's King David invaded Northumberland and, though beaten at the Battle of the Standards, was able to take advantage of the dynastic chaos in England to negotiate terms that gave him Cumberland and Northumberland. For the next 20 years the Scots, not the Normans, held sway in both areas and Northumberland's nobility, who had sided with the Scots in the invasion, remained culturally closer to Scotland than to Norman England.

Richard Lomas (*County of Conflict: Northumberland from Conquest to Civil War*) explains that this was unsurprising as there were no significant differences of race, language and way of life between Scotland and Northumberland. The French-speaking barons of the latter were just "as willing to accept a French-speaking king of Scotland as a French-speaking king of England".

In 1157 the English under the redoubtable Henry II succeeded in re-establishing authority over Northumberland and in 1237 the border was mutually agreed by the Treaty of York, which gave the Scots some land in Cumberland in return for renunciation of their claim to Northumberland.

The Tweed became the border, with some minor variations.

The period between 1157 and 1296 was a happy one for Northumberland in which there was comparative peace, and its towns prospered. Agriculture flourished, the population grew, vast sheep flocks were built up, and a healthy export trade to Europe of wool and cloth (thanks to the new spinning wheel) was developed. Most notably, there was also an extensive program of ecclesiastical building.

In 1294 the Scots removed their king, John Balliol (Jean de Bailleu), a Norman-French magnate with vast lands in France, England and (then only by marriage) Scotland. This was their first mistake, as the ruthless English king, Edward I, had put John on the throne. Their second was to conclude an alliance with Edward's mortal enemy, France, in 1295. In March 1296 Edward seized Berwick-upon-Tweed, butchering 7000 (some historians say more) of its inhabitants. This was a calculated outrage by Edward to impress on the Scots the dreadful price they would pay if they resisted him. It worked. Scottish

King Edward 1
'Longshanks'
1239-1307

resistance evaporated after the defeat of a Scots army at Dunbar, and Edward was able quickly to bring Scotland to heel.

But the Scots are a spirited people. The occupation of Scotland, and the brutality of its occupiers, unleashed a campaign of Scottish resistance that has become a matter of legend (including Hollywood). In 1297 William Wallace won a major victory at Stirling Bridge, but in the next year lost, and was captured at, a battle at Falkirk. Resistance continued and nearly every year between 1297 and 1307 Edward was forced to bring an army into Scotland. Northumberland suffered severely during this period as the Scots responded with savage raids into its territory.

Until his death in 1307, Edward prevailed against the Scots; a brutal and driven man, he was a formidable general with a burning desire to bring Scotland to heel. But his son, Edward II, was made of lesser stuff. In addition, in 1306, Scotland had a new king, Robert Bruce, who proved to be both an effective national leader and successful soldier. There was also a stiffening of the Scottish spine as the notion of nationhood started to prevail over self-interest and expediency.

In 1314 Robert Bruce defeated the English at Bannockburn and secured Edward II's recognition of Scotland as a fully independent kingdom. From then, until his death in 1328, Bruce gave almost incessant attention to Northumberland; in so doing, according to Lomas, he was to "inflict upon Northumberland the darkest and most miserable conditions it has ever had to endure". This constant harassment (in conjunction with harvest failures) led to massive loss of income by estates and churches, destruction of buildings and population decline due to death and flight.

The death of 'The Bruce' led, between 1333 and 1377, to a resurgence of English authority over Scotland but thereafter the Scots gradually expelled the English. One by one the last remaining English-held castles in southern Scotland fell to the Scots, the last, Roxburgh Castle, in 1460. Only Berwick-upon-Tweed remained in English hands – doing so permanently after being formally ceded by the Scots in 1482.

In this turbulent and bloody period, Northumberland continued to be a battleground on which Scots and English forces fought causing great suffering to its economy and people. Some, though, did well. The devolution of responsibility for Border defence to regional forces made powerful local leadership essential. This enabled the rise to power of several families, most notably the Percys, who by 1400 had emerged as the dominant landowner and holders of the earldom of Northumberland.

However, during this time a new menace emerged to threaten the peace, security and economy of Northumberland: the border raiders (or *reivers*). Motivated by plunder, rather than territorial aspirations, the Scottish raiders travelled south through the Cheviots to steal and burn deep into Northumberland, and sometimes as far as Yorkshire. A similar motive, and route, took Northumberland raiders into southern Scotland. Thus it was that cross-border theft provided support for a precarious border economy, and in the process on either side of the Cheviots, perhaps as much as ten per cent of the landmass of Britain, a society was created that existed outside the laws of either nation.

Etching from J. M.W. Turner's painting of Norham Castle

Norham Castle is situated on a promontory of the River Tweed, and is one of the most impressive medieval castles in England. It was built in 1121 and was besieged many times, becoming known as 'the most dangerous place in England'. In 1513 it was stormed and taken by James IV Scotland just before his defeat at Flodden.

If all this wasn't enough, Northumberland became a major theatre in the Wars of the Roses in which the Lancastrian forces first prevailed but finally succumbed in 1485 to the House of York. In this time, Alnwick, Dunstanburgh, Warkworth, Norham and Bamburgh castles changed hands on a number of occasions. However, thankfully, this war had relatively little impact on the general population, being principally a battle between nobles and their armies.

In 1513 Scotland agreed to a French request that it distract Henry VIII from his campaign in France by mounting a diversion in England's north. While a desire to help the French was a powerful motivation, there can be little doubt that smouldering Scottish enmity towards England was the main reason for this very unwise decision. It led James IV to Flodden Field.

The site of this battle on a hillside field in Northumberland is perhaps the most evocative symbol of the warring between England and Scotland. In this, the "greatest military defeat Scotland ever suffered, led with folly", James lost his life, his heir, about 10,000 men, 12 Scottish earls, 15 lords and chieftains, assorted bishops and abbots, and his reputation. Given the scale of this defeat it's amazing that James V repeated the mistake of his predecessor; in 1542 he invaded England with a large army, only to be utterly routed at Solway Moss.

However, English fear of invasion by the Scots, supported by their French allies, remained and the border defences were reconstructed accordingly, the most impressive being the fortifications of Berwick-upon-Tweed.

Given this terrible period of violence it is not surprising that the once great Northumberland entered the 17th Century in a sorry state. John Talbot White (*The Scottish Border and Northumberland*) summarized the situation well: "The constant raiding which came to a climax in the 16th Century had a devastating impact on Border life and led to the depopulation of many of the more vulnerable areas and to the lack of large, prosperous villages".

The raiders were largely subdued by James I of England (VI of Scotland) after the Union of the Two Crowns in 1603. By 1609 the Borders were purged "of all the chiefest malefactors, robbers and brigands". Sporadic raiding was to continue but it was localized and on a small scale, and finally petered out as the economy of the borders mended.

Parliamentary cavalry fording the Tyne at Newburn

Scottish armies fought with the Parliamentary cause in the English Civil War during which they captured Charles I and surrendered him to the English Parliamentarians (and with his execution lost their King as well). Half a decade later the Scots were at war with Cromwell after they crowned Charles II King of Scotland, and were twice soundly defeated. Until the restoration of the monarchy, Scotland remained under the sway of Cromwell's New Model Army.

Thereafter, apart from the futile Jacobite rebellions of 1715 and 1745 (which prompted the building of the military road – now the B6318 – and the barracks at Berwick-upon-Tweed), the two countries, enemies for over

500 years, were at peace.

The centuries of bloody battles have been to the visitors' advantage as they can now view the many fortifications that such troubled times necessitated. In fact, Northumberland has more castles than any other county in the British Isles as well as numerous lesser fortifications such as pele towers and bastle houses, fortified dwellings built to protect livestock and people from Scottish raiders.

REVOLUTIONS OF THE BLOODLESS SORT

Obviously Northumberland's history did not stop after the troubles with Scotland, but it was the close of the 'blood and guts' chapter. What followed was a new period of turmoil as Northumberland experienced two revolutions that would radically change the face of its agricultural and industrial life.

By the time order was restored in Northumberland, the world had changed; demand for agricultural produce from within Britain and from abroad had increased, bringing with it the opportunity for profit. But before the opportunity could be taken an overhaul of traditional farming practices was required, as had occurred much earlier in the south of Britain. In this way, the agricultural 'revolution' reached Northumberland. Medieval subsistence farming was no longer appropriate to the demands of the new marketplace. It was time, as John Talbot White explains, "to construct a new landscape in place of the old". This the local landowners set about doing with gusto, starting in the 17th Century and with accelerating haste in the next. This process was facilitated by the availability of large areas of fertile land in Northumberland, concentrated in the hands of a few large landholders.

Medieval ploughland was enclosed with hedgerows or stone walls and aggregated into larger properties; land was drained and reclaimed; lime was used to 'sweeten' the soil; the practice of crop rotation was introduced to maintain productive capability; new crops and new breeds of livestock were introduced; new ploughing techniques, and new ploughs, came into use and large areas of land (at least 60,000 acres) previously covered in gorse and broom were cleared and brought into productive use. By the 19th Century only the poor moorland pasture on high ground was left unfenced for use as common grazing land and Northumberland had a national reputation as a county of agricultural innovation.

This came at a cost. Many former farm tenants were dispossessed to find their livelihoods, or to despair, in towns. Old villages were destroyed and replaced by fewer estate settlements designed to house agricultural workers. While a number of 'model' villages were created (such as those at Blanchland, Cambo, Etal and Ford) to provide decent housing, safe water and schools, agricultural reforms generally did not provide improvements in human lives; the mass of the labour force continued to be victims of poverty and deprivation.

There were other changes to the landscape as ease took priority over defence. New, more comfortable dwellings were built, including a number of grand houses; existing grand houses and castles were renovated; large areas of manor parkland were created and other open areas re-forested (together entailing the planting of nearly two million trees). New churches were built and old ones restored; a new road system was built by turnpike trusts (between 1746 and 1826, nineteen trusts controlled 500 miles of Northumberland's roads), along with new bridges. By the mid 18th Century, surfaced roads linked all main towns.

To better handle the movement of agricultural produce, ports were improved and developed as at Alnmouth, Seahouses, and Berwick-upon-Tweed. A fishing industry developed from harbours such as Holy Island,

Blyth, Seahouses and Newbiggin-by-the-Sea.

At the same time some market towns, notably Alnwick, Morpeth and Berwick-upon-Tweed, were rebuilt and developed as administrative and market centres, but many villages slipped quietly into decline, being no longer required in the new agricultural order. Even towns like Bamburgh and Warkworth were preserved "almost fossil like in the bedrock of (their) past".

The devastation and depopulation of Northumberland over centuries allowed those with wealth and power to acquire vast tracts of land that they held with an iron grip. What's more, rather than dispose of land during the settled times, these large landowners further increased their holdings to allow them greater productive efficiency. As John Talbot White noted: "The landscape of Northumberland is pre-eminently a landlord-created landscape. [They] used their power to build, enclose, hedge, drain and plant – and to evict. They transformed a generally desolate and neglected countryside". Thus it was that a determined and energetic period of estate-building led to the accumulation of enormous land holdings by a few notable owners.

The rural landscape we see today in Northumberland is the product of this period of transformation; one stark feature most evident to the visitor is that it is "a landscape without people". Already depopulated by centuries of war and raiding, Northumberland saw many of its agricultural workers displaced in the 17th and 18th Centuries. By the mid 19th Century roughly half the rural population was lost to the cities, principally Newcastle-upon-Tyne, a drift away from agriculture that continues today.

While the agricultural 'revolution' was transforming the countryside, another 'revolution' was transforming Newcastle and its environs. This *industrial* revolution had its genesis in the rich coal resources of Tyneside, arguably

23

Coal Staithes

Britain's most important supplier of coal. First developed as an industry by the need for coal for heating and cooking in London, when timber supplies were depleted in Tudor times, the coal industry of Tyneside boomed in the 18th and 19th Centuries and continued until the last quarter of the 20th Century. This trade led in time to the development of railways, first to carry the coal from the mines to the Tyne for loading in ships, and later to link towns throughout Northumberland.

At first the shallow seams were mined, but as they ran out and demand increased, underground deposits had to be exploited. And here technology came to the rescue: important developments included steam engines that pumped water from the deep chambers and lifted coal to the surface, underground haulage engines and the safety lamp. All of this required a new industry: iron manufacturing to make the mining machinery and the rails and locomotive engines that linked the mines and took the coal to the ports.

This industrial base was fortuitous because it coincided with the demands for rail and locomotive machinery that accompanied the growth of the railway system that by the mid 19th Century was spreading throughout the rest of Britain. Newcastle factories became important producers of rails and locomotives and sections for iron bridges.

More ship builders established their yards in Tyneside in the second half of

HMS Victoria, 1888

the 19th Century and these gradually occupied much of the riverside. One of the finest testaments to the skill of the shipbuilders was the grand liner, *Mauretania*, launched in 1907. Chemical and electrical engineering were among the other great industries that joined those already established, drawn as by a magnet to its technological expertise and close supply of coal.

At the start of this industrial era, Newcastle was a relatively small walled city. It emerged at the end a true, multifaceted megalopolis that was to

Iron and Coal
by William Bell Scott,
a tapestry painting
which can be seen at
Wallington Hall,
near Morpeth

contribute significantly to Britain's industrial expansion. The wealth it generated accelerated the construction of grand country houses such as

Longhirst, Linden and Matfen Halls (all later to provide the grounds for fine golf courses). At the other end of the socio-economic scale were the modest terraced houses still so typical of the residential landscape of Newcastle and its dormitory towns such as Blyth and Ashington. Sadly, industrialization was achieved at a heavy human cost in mines and factories where conditions were generally intolerable. These were only ameliorated – and then only very slowly – after the growth of trade unions after 1831 and the public outrage over a number of horrific mine disasters.

But this should not obscure us to the fact that Tyneside remains a monument to the industrial genius personalized by George Stephenson, "the father of (British) railways" and inventor of the *Rocket* locomotive, his son, Robert, also a great engineer, and Charles Parsons who developed the steam turbine for power stations and ships' engines. Perhaps the greatest of the Victorian industrialists was William George (Lord) Armstrong who abandoned a legal career in the 1850s to found W G Armstrong and Company which, from its works at Elswick on the outskirts of Newcastle, manufactured a wide range of equipment and machinery, including steam engines, dock gates and hydraulic cranes, and later military ordnance.

Charles Parsons
1854-1931

Robert Stephenson
1903-1859

Lord Armstrong
1810-1900

The Elswick factory has been described as "one of the greatest engineering enterprises of the day, giving employment to nearly 4000 men".

Tyneside's period of industrial greatness was, as John Talbot White says, "not only [dependent on] a happy conjunction of natural resources such as abundance of coal and deep estuary, but on the quality and invention of its people".

The era of prosperity and growth did not last. After its height during World War I, recession was followed by a depression in the 1930s that resulted in 50 per cent to 75 per cent of the workforce being thrown out of work. There was recovery after Britain re-armed after the late 1930s, but after World War II the coal industry was nationalized and pits were closed as the demand for coal diminished. Shipbuilding and other heavy industries experienced a matching decline in the face of foreign competition. By the 1960s, the shipbuilding industry had been lost and Northumberland's other traditional heavy industries were in terminal decline.

However, Newcastle is now finding new sources of wealth and employment, and its urban renewal is evidence of a new spirit, and a new prosperity, unsurprising given its proven capacity to adapt and to innovate.

Gone are the days of the grim and blackened industrial quayside.
Today the banks of the Tyne are a focal point of culture and recreation.

So, what has this revolutionary period meant to the visitor? We would argue, not much. Despite all the turmoil of the centuries, Northumberland has retained its wilderness areas, its rural character, its magnificent coastline, and its historic monuments. It has a modern history, but thankfully one that spared its beauty. Insofar as damage has been done to the environment and amenity of Northumberland by industrialisation, it remains in one small corner to the southeast.

Thus we leave our story of Northumberland's rich history with a reminder to the reader that it is only a sample to whet the appetite. We have been deliberately selective, for otherwise we would have had to write a history book which others more competent have already written.

THE VIRTUE OF ENGAGING SETTLEMENTS AND PLACES

Set among the lovely countryside of Northumberland are numerous picturesque villages, towns and sites of interest. For us, these constitute Northumberland's third 'virtue'.

Yes, we know that Britain is covered in picturesque settlements and interesting sites and, yes, there may be some prettier villages, more impressive castles and grander houses to be found elsewhere. But we argue that Northumberland has several distinct advantages:

First, the county's settlements and sites include a number that have no equivalent in the rest of Britain. We contend that, for example, Hadrian's Wall and Holy Island are unique, while sites such as Chew Green and Yeavering Bell have a special magic. These locate you in ancient and significant places that have enough of their original fabric remaining to stir powerful emotions. It's this assault on the imagination that we found compelling, and we consider it will have wide appeal to other visitors.

Second, as mentioned earlier, all the attractions we offer are contained in a reasonably compact area and are easily accessible to the visitor. There are no urban obstacles to movement around the county, and the roads and places of interest are uncongested. It is a simple truth that a visitor to Northumberland will see and do more in any one time than is possible anywhere else in Britain.

The last advantage is that because of its history, small population and retained rural character, Northumberland is free of the ugliness and human congestion that is a common, and inevitable consequence of an industrial past and modern development found in other areas of tourist interest. There is no unsightly residue from industry, bygone or present. There are no vast shopping centres, expanses of architecturally uninspired 'new towns' and blocks of decaying high-rise buildings to distract the observer from the essential beauty of its attractions. The market towns still look much as they did 300 years ago while the pretty stone villages are preserved with modern additions complementing, not marring, the original architecture.

Thus it is that the attractions of Northumberland offer a scenic as well as an emotional dividend, are freely available to the visitor even on a short visit, and lie among a backdrop of preserved beauty and tranquility.

What we present now is an introduction to a selection of Northumberland's many engaging settlements and sites. We have been deliberate in choosing a small number of personal favourites as examples of the type of places on offer to the visitor. Visitors will find their own special places as they journey through the county, just as those now described were found by us. You can be assured there is plenty to choose from.

ALNMOUTH

Alnmouth (pronounced "Alanmouth"), a pretty seaside town located on the mouth of the River Aln, was once a prosperous grain port and shipbuilding

centre. It dates from 1150 with the foundation deed executed in Edinburgh in the court of William the Lion. During the Middle Ages it served as the main seaport for the area but in 1806 a great storm changed the course of the river, and ended its days as a port. A completely irrelevant piece of information is that John Paul Jones, the Scot who founded the American navy, bombarded the port during the American War of Independence.

Today only yachts and small craft lie in the Aln estuary. The ruin of the Norman church of St Waleric, on Church Hill on the south side of the Aln (accessible only through dunes), stands on the site of an Anglo-Saxon church. Alnmouth's nine-hole links golf course is one of the oldest in England, being first laid out in 1869. Alnmouth is a lovely spot to walk around and enjoy views of the sea and estuary and old buildings, and to embark on beautiful coastal walks.

ALNWICK

Alnwick (in this case pronounced "Annick") is an attractive, stone-built market town that deserves its recent recognition as the best place to live in Britain. Its lovely cobbled market square retains its medieval character with narrow streets and lanes radiating out in all directions. Dominating the market place is the Northumberland Hall built in 1826 – the old town hall built fifty years earlier stands to its side. The main gateway to the market square is the Hotspur Tower, built in 1450 as part of the town's (now lost) walls. To the east of the town centre is the Percy Tenantry Column erected in 1816 by tenants grateful to the second Duke for a 25 per cent rent reduction because of the hardships of the Napoleonic Wars.

Alnwick has many original 18th and 19th Century buildings; cosy pubs; an old-world hotel with a grand dining room taken from the *Olympic,* the sister

ship of the *Titanic;* a wonderful playhouse; the largest second-hand bookshop in Britain housed in the old stone railway station and the House of Hardy, whose famous fishing tackle is exported all over the world. The Church of St Michael (above) is the finest perpendicular church in Northumberland and dates from a complete reconstruction carried out after 1464.

The town is dominated by the greatest of the border fortresses, Alnwick Castle, still the home of the Percy family whose ancestors ruled much of northern England for most of the Middle Ages. Until the Wars of the Roses – when it was besieged and taken several times – Alnwick Castle was given a wide berth by enemy forces respectful of its formidable defensive strength and the military force within. This truly awesome Castle stands nobly above the River Aln and occupies an area of seven acres. It is entered from the town by an impressive barbican and gatehouse dating from the early 14th Century; its battlements are adorned with remarkable carved stone 'sentries' of 18th Century origin but probably replacing much earlier figures.

The original castle developed from a motte and bailey structure to a stone castle between 1090 and 1157 and was then substantially re-built by Henry de Percy between 1309 and 1315. Henry's great grandson was created Earl of Northumberland and thereafter the castle passed to eleven generations of Percy earls. When the male Percy line died out, the Castle passed to Sir Hugh Smithson in 1750 who took the Percy name and, in 1766, was created 1st *Duke* of Northumberland. At the time the Castle was in poor repair.

Alnwick Castle, an unfamiliar view

The 1ˢᵗ Duke commissioned the noted architect James Paine to rebuild the castle's exterior and the even more renowned Robert Adam to do the internal redecoration. In this period the great English landscape architect, Lancelot "Capability" Brown, was engaged to lay out sections of the castle's grounds. A further phase of restoration work was undertaken in the 1850s by the greatest of the Victorian Gothic castle architects, Salvin, to reflect the 4th Duke's love of Renaissance Italian art and decoration. It is Salvin's restoration and interpretation of a medieval fortress that we see today – Adam's interiors are no more.

Alnwick Castle retains its imposing and largely unchanged exterior, thereby making it much sought after by film producers seeking an authentic period location (most recently for the films *Elizabeth* and the *Harry Potter* series).

Looking up from the Lion Bridge (built in 1773) over the Aln, you have a view of the Castle little different from those of the eye of an 18th Century passer-by. But the exterior is well matched by the castle's interior where many treasures are to be found, including arms and armour; artwork by Titian, Raphael, Van Dyck, Turner, Kneller, Canaletto and Gainsborough; fine furniture; wood panelling; marble statues; thousands of antique books and damask hangings. Among these treasures are found the personal possessions of the Percy family acquired over centuries, for the visitor is invited into a home, not a museum.

In addition to the main Castle building, there are three towers of particular interest for both their contents and their architecture – they have been little altered since they were first built in the 14th Century. The Constable's Tower contains a rare armoury; the Postern Tower houses a museum of British and Roman archaeological artifacts and the Abbot's Tower houses the regimental museum of the Royal Northumberland Fusiliers.

Twelve acres of the castle's gardens have been redeveloped by the Duchess of Northumberland around striking water features intended to turn the grounds into "Britain's answer to Versailles". The centrepiece is the Grand Cascade, where every minute 7200 gallons of water flow down enormous steps, and fountains periodically spray water six metres into the air. A more recent addition is an enormous wooden tree house, said to be the largest in Europe.

Attached to the Castle are 3000 acres of land enclosed by a wall stretching over nine miles in length. A section of the estate, Hulne Park, is open to visitors and offers superb walks through mature woodland running along the valley of the Aln. The attractions of the Park are both natural and man-made. Included in the former is the abundant wildlife, including pheasants, squirrels and grey deer, and the thick woods and streams. The man-made attractions include the well-preserved ruins of Hulne Priory,

Remains of Hulne Priory

founded in the mid 13th Century for the Carmelites, and its 15th Century pele tower; the 14th Century fortified gateway to what had been an Abbey founded in 1147 and the ornate Brizlee Tower, built 90 feet high in 1781 to a design by Robert Adam.

BAMBURGH

Bamburgh, to the north along the coast from Alnmouth, was once the ancient capital of Northumbria and the residence of its kings. Dominating this pretty village from its 150 foot high vantage point on the Whin Sill is Bamburgh Castle, the most spectacularly sited castle in Northumberland, occupying over eight acres of land. It isn't the first fortification on this site: there was an Iron Age hill fort there on which, in 547AD, the Anglo-Saxons built a wooden fort and royal palace. In 537AD the Saxon king Ethelfrith gave the settlement to his wife Bebba, from which it derives its name "Bebban-burgh". In 993AD the town was sacked by the Danes and remained a ruin until William the Conqueror built a small wooden fort on the site.

The origins of the current castle are not clear, but a fortification of substance was clearly established in the 11th Century. The 78 foot high keep was probably built in the mid 12th Century. Repairs were done in the 1330s and major building work undertaken in the 1380s.

The castle has seen several sieges, the last in 1463 during the Wars of the Roses when it achieved the dubious distinction of being the first castle in England to be taken by cannon fire. Afterwards it suffered considerable neglect and in 1538 was described as being in a state of ruin and decay. Extensive restoration took place between the 1750s and early years of the 19th Century but it fell into disrepair again. In 1884 the castle was purchased by the great industrialist Lord Armstrong who had it rebuilt, completing the work in 1903. Despite this 'modern' architectural imposition, Bamburgh still presents an awesome picture of medieval strength from afar.

The most impressive part of the castle is the keep with its stone-roofed armoury and a huge collection of armour and firearms. On the ground floor is a well dating from Saxon times, bored to a depth of 140 feet through sandstone and basalt. The 19th Century Kings's Hall has a carved teak roof and a display of armour and firearms. Among the treasures are a magnificent library, rare furniture, china and porcelain and wonderful engravings and portraits. There is also a museum commemorating the formidable industrial achievements of Lord Armstrong.

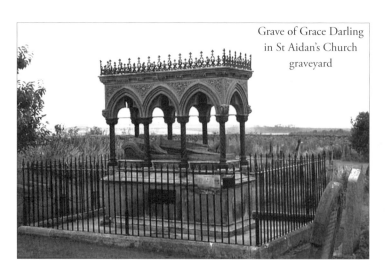

Grave of Grace Darling
in St Aidan's Church
graveyard

In the village of Bamburgh is the parish church of St Aidan, one of the finest of its type in Britain and said to have been built on the site of a Saxon church where St Aidan died in 651AD. The large nave and square tower, and the vaulted crypt were built in the 13th Century. The crypt has two chambers separated by a wall into which a Saxon sundial has been set.

BERWICK-UPON-TWEED

Berwick, set high above the mouth of the River Tweed, is the most northerly town in England, and the most impressive town in Northumberland. For centuries it was on the front line of the wars between Scotland and England. Sadly, Berwick-upon-Tweed's original 12th Century castle, the place of so much bloody history, is no more. First mentioned in 1160, it was rebuilt by Edward I in 1296. It was abandoned in the 17th Century and its stones taken by locals for building material. What was left was largely demolished to build the town's railway station. All that remains today are one of its towers (the Constable Tower) and a little of the original wall.

Bridges at Berwick

Nevertheless, Berwick has beautifully preserved fortified walls built between 1558 and 1569 by Elizabeth I to protect the town from the threat of Franco-Scottish invasion ("the costliest undertaking of the Queen's reign"). The walls are said to "represent the apex of the art of fortification and are unique in Europe", being the first specifically designed by two Italian engineers to exploit and neutralise artillery. Running for 1.5 miles, they offer fine views of the harbour at the mouth of the Tweed, the town and the coast.

In addition Berwick has an impressive 18th Century town hall, military barracks designed by Sir John Vanburgh built in 1721 and four imposing bridges over the Tweed. The oldest of these, completed between 1619 and 1624 on the order of James VI of Scotland, is of red sandstone with fifteen arches. Another, the Royal Border Bridge, built by Robert Stephenson, was opened in 1850 and has 28 arches carrying the railway. It's said to be "the greatest engineering achievement of its time".

It's not only its awesome structures that give Berwick its magic – this comes with recognition of its centrality and suffering in the wars between Scotland and England during which the town changed hands fourteen times between 1147 and 1482. As mentioned before, but worth repeating, is that in one dreadful event, Edward I slaughtered 7000 inhabitants and left their bodies in the streets to rot to intimidate the Scottish lords summoned to accept his authority. Its history and geography has left Berwick with a dual personality: politically part of Northumberland since 1482, it is culturally more Scottish.

Indeed Berwick's status as a "free burgh" granted in the 16th Century, placed it for a time outside the sovereign territory of both Scotland and England. In 1853 war was declared on Russia in the name of "Victoria, Queen of Great Britain, Ireland, Berwick-upon-Tweed and all other British Dominions". When peace was declared in 1856 no mention was made of Berwick in the treaty – technically the town remained at war with Russia.

This was not corrected until 1966 when the town signed a peace treaty with the USSR, at which time the Berwick mayor made the observation that "the people of Russia can at last sleep easy in their beds".

CHEW GREEN

Chew Green, only a short drive from Rothbury via Alwinton, is the remains of a substantial Roman camp (*Ad Finis* , or "the end of the world") on the upper reaches of Coquetdale at a height of 1400 feet. This sits on the side of the route of Dere Street, a main, paved road running across most difficult and remote terrain from Corbridge on the Wall to the Eildon Hills in Scotland.

There are two reasons for visiting Chew Green. One is the lovely drive from Rothbury through the Northumberland National Park along the banks of the River Coquet into the Cheviot Hills. You will enjoy the long views of moorland, river valley and farmland.

The other reason is to be impressed further by what an eminent historian describes as "the most remarkable visible group of Roman earthworks in Britain". Here you can see plainly the outline of two rectangular camps, one 900 feet square containing a strong fort 250 feet square with triple ramparts, and a labour camp 500 feet square. At one point, just to the side of the camp as you approach it uphill along a path from the south, you can make out drainage ditches on both sides of what had been the path of Dere Street. This is a place of desolate beauty, history and atmosphere, and a further reminder of the engineering skills of the formidable Romans.

CHILLINGHAM CASTLE

Chillingham Castle, the ancestral home between 1695 and 1931 of the Earl of Tankerville, was completed in 1348. It stands on the site of an earlier castle largely destroyed by Scottish raiders in around 1296; the south west tower of the current structure is said to have been part of the original structure. The 'new' castle was damaged by artillery in 1536 but was repaired thereafter. Major alterations were undertaken in the early 17th Century, in part to give it a grander appearance. Following the death of the seventh earl in 1931 the castle was abandoned and its contents sold. Used as barracks during the Second World War, the garrison, and later wet and dry rot, destroyed much of its interior. Since 1980 the castle has been subject to extensive restoration by Sir Humphry Wakefield.

With its distinctive four square corner towers constructed around an old pele tower, Chillingham is said to be the county's finest 14th Century castle. The Great Hall, with its stone flooring, armour and arrow slits, was used for interior scenes in the film *Elizabeth*. There is a museum and a cellar transformed into a 'torture chamber'.

The castle's gardens were originally laid out in around 1828 by Sir Jeffrey Wyatville who was responsible for the grounds of Windsor Castle. Later neglected, they were restored in 1986 by Isobel Murray, a local amateur landscape gardener, in what has been described as "a masterpiece of restoration".

Nearby Chillingham Park (365 acres) is famous as the home of a herd of wild white cattle, the sole survivors of a species descended from British wild oxen which roamed the forested hills of northern Britain as early as the Bronze Age. The herd has remained pure for nearly 800 years having been isolated in the park when it was enclosed in 1220.

CRAGSIDE HOUSE

This property, the creation of Lord Armstrong, lies on the outskirts of Rothbury. Setting out to achieve a personal paradise, Armstrong started in 1863 with a modest hunting lodge and 20 acres of land on a moorland hillside and finished in 1884 with a dramatic Victorian country house and a well-wooded picturesque estate of over 1700 acres. Using the technological genius that had made him an industrial Great, he created an extensive hydraulic system to pump water, turn spits, power a saw mill and farm machinery, and run a dynamo producing electric light (Cragside was the first house in the world to be lit by hydroelectricity).

Armstrong built lakes, planted an extensive range of shrubs and trees (predominantly conifers) and a large rock garden with rocks manhandled into position. A contemporary description of his achievement was this: "Words are inadequate to describe the wonderful transformation…made on the barren hill-side as it existed previously to 1863. Every natural advantage has been utilized by the great magician. Shrubs and trees that grow best in exposed situations have been planted among the boulders of Cragside with admirable results. Rhododendrons, azaleas, and other plants of rich coloured bloom, with native heather, bracken and ling, soften and brighten the hard features of the landscape till it smiles again".

The transformation of the house was equally impressive. The small lodge was extended and rebuilt into a remarkable manor. It's filled with wonderful carved panels, stained glass, antiques, works of art, ornate ceilings, and in the drawing room a massive, carved Italian marble fireplace, and even Armstrong's butterfly and stuffed bird collections.

Also in the grounds is the Tumbleton Ram House located on a lake created by the damming of the Debdon burn which runs through the property. This houses a hydraulic engine that powered the pumps that pushed water up to a reservoir 200 feet above the house. The water flowing down provided the house's hydraulic power.

DUNSTANBURGH CASTLE

This wonderful edifice was completed in 1319 on an outcrop of the Great Whin Sill. It is reached by a short walk from Craster, an unspoilt fishing village overlooking a tiny harbour. Its small local fleet fishes for crab, lobster, and salmon, and the village is famous for its smoked kippers, to which the constant, but not unpleasant, odour of the process attests.

The castle was built by the Earl of Lancaster (cousin of Edward II) who

employed the services of a master mason trained by James of Gordon, Edward 1's master castle builder. Under the ownership of John of Gaunt (son of Edward III and father of Henry IV), the Castle was radically strengthened in the 1380s. It fell into disrepair in the early decades of the 14th Century but was repaired thereafter, just in time to do service in the Wars of the Roses during which the castle changed hands between Yorkist and Lancastrian forces five times. By 1550 it was a ruin and a source of stone for local builders.

Dunstanburgh rises 100 feet sheer from the sea and has superb coastal views, including of the local bird life nesting on the cliffs. Covering eleven acres there are impressive remains of the curtain wall, three towers and a massive gatehouse. The castle is a favourite local attraction, especially for walkers who can smugly observe the travails of golfers attempting a difficult shot over the sea on the 13th hole of the Dunstanburgh Golf Club, to our mind the county's second best links course.

THE FARNE ISLANDS

The 28 or so Farne Islands lie off the coast from the small port of Seahouses and are accessible using one of the many sightseeing boats that operate in summer. Formed by the final outlier of the Great Whin Sill, they rise sharply and starkly from the ocean and are quite splendid to see from the sea. They are home to a wonderful array of birds, including puffins, eider ducks, cormorants, terns, kittiwakes, guillemots, razorbills, and to Atlantic grey seals.

However, the natural beauty of the islands is complemented by man-made attractions. The most prominent is Longstone lighthouse perched on a rocky reef off the Inner Farne (16 acres at low water with cliffs 80 feet high). Built in 1826, Longstone is notable for once being the home of Grace Darling, arguably the world's first media-created heroine, who in 1839 rowed with her father a mile across rough seas to rescue survivors of a ship that had run aground on a nearby island. Another less prominent, but far prettier, lighthouse was built high on the cliffs of Inner Farne in 1808. Both lighthouses still operate today but are now automatic.

In addition, there is a complex of medieval monastic buildings on Inner Farne inspired by the island's connection with St Cuthbert (who lived there for six years before his death in 687). In 1370 St Cuthbert's Church was built incorporating much older masonry, perhaps dating from the 1240s. The Church was restored in the 19th Century by the then Archdeacon of Durham Cathedral, Charles Thorp. Included in this restoration were the church's wonderful woodwork, pews, and a 15th Century font, all of which came from the Cathedral. Nearby is a stone tower built in 1500 by monks as a defensive residence. Originally a rough structure, it was softened by 18th Century additions such as its balustrade, woodwork and fireplaces.

FLODDEN FIELD

Flodden, an open field on Branxton Moor just outside the village of Branxton, may seem a strange place to be included on a list of favourites. A visit will soon show the reason. Make the effort to walk to the simple but moving monument at the site of the last great battle between Scotland and England: it reads "Flodden 1513: To the Brave of Both Nations". Reflect here on the awesome loss of life and its profound impact at the time on the fabric of Scotland. As they say here, "nought else to say". As with Holy Island, this is a place that relies on atmosphere to have its impact on the visitor.

Take time to visit the austere but serene St Paul's Church down from the Field on the outskirts of Branxton. This sits on the site of a 12th Century church where the body of James IV lay after the battle. It was rebuilt in 1849 with only the Chancel Arch remaining of the Norman church. It's one of our favourite Northumbrian churches because of its beautifully simple proportions.

HADRIAN'S WALL

The Wall is without doubt Northumberland's principal man-made attraction. While we can't say that it is, as claimed, the "greatest monument to Roman civilization in Europe", it's certainly the best testament to Roman glory in Britain. It's said that in its heyday, the Wall was second only to the Great Wall of China.

The Wall was begun in 122 AD on the orders of the Emperor Hadrian and finished eight years later by a work force of 10,000 men. Its vital statistics are breathtaking: it stretches 73 miles from the estuaries of the Tyne in the east to the Solway Firth in the west; was built ten feet wide and fifteen feet high from four million tonnes of stone and other building material, and was strengthened at key points by forts, milecastles and turrets. The whole length was fronted to the north by a V-shaped ditch 27 feet wide and ten feet deep. To the south was a *vallum*, a broad ditch about 120 yards wide and ten feet deep crossed by causeways. This was the southern edge of the military zone, a sort of customs zone. A paved road ran between the Wall and the *vallum* linking the forts and milecastles. For 275 years the Wall remained the most northerly boundary of the Roman Empire except when between 139 to 163 its place was taken by a stone and turf wall between the Firths of Forth and Clyde.

Though it had a clear, defensive function, its primary purpose was, according to Hunter Davies (*A Walk Along the Wall*), "to lay out an unmistakable marker of the Empire's jurisdiction and to set up a system of frontier traffic control". By its presence and function, Barbarians from the north could be detected and controlled.

Though for centuries a convenient quarry for dressed stones for local buildings, sections of the Wall (described in one Saxon poem as "works of giants crumbling") retain their grandeur, especially where altitude and isolation have deterred large-scale appropriation of its structure.

Walking on the Wall, as you can do on many sections (with the finest at Housesteads), you can't help marvelling at Roman engineering genius, organizational skills and perseverance. The sheer magnitude of the undertaking stirs the imagination. Looking out over the bleak (but beautiful) landscape, still isolated today, you can't help asking what must the cold and isolated Roman soldiers have felt when on duty, watching out for those who would fight them so ferociously.

There are four archeological sites along the Wall that reveal much of the life and times of their Roman garrisons. These are the remains of the

Roman forts and associated civil settlements at Vindolanda, Housesteads, Corbridge and Chesters. In the forts, that cover four to six acres, you can see evidence of centrally heated bathhouses, water distribution systems, latrines, granaries, stables, administrative buildings, barracks, storehouses, gates, shrines and temples, all of which afford a good insight into the life of the garrisons that occupied them. There is less in evidence of the structures of the civil settlements but nevertheless there are remains of houses, shops, storehouses, shops and taverns.

Roman Bath House, Chesters

Vindolanda was built on the site of several earlier forts around 300 with later rebuilding about 70 years later. The adjourning civil settlement covered about ten acres. In addition to the usual displays, Vindolanda has remains of a system used to pipe water to its major buildings and substantial remains of the fort walls ranging in height from six to ten feet. This shows a variety of stonework attributed to repairs over time. Further, it has reconstructions of the turf and timber walls of the early forts and of stone walls, with tower, of the later. There is also a collection of full-sized replica Roman buildings.

Housesteads, which dates from 120, is the best known and most complete

Roman fort in Britain. It's also the most dramatic, sitting on a commanding position on the Whin Sill. It has particularly well preserved remains of a fort gate and latrines. Six buildings from the civil settlement are also on display.

Corbridge was located strategically at the point where Dere Street crossed the Tyne and intersected Stanegate (the main road west to Carlisle). The fort was in service for about 40 years after around 122 but was decommissioned and replaced with a town covering twenty-seven acres. In addition to all the displays found in wall forts, Corbridge has a section of Stanegate and a fine example of a fountain house, the distribution point for public water supply.

Chesters sits on the bank of the North Tyne north of Hexham and covers nearly six acres. In addition to all that the other sites show, it has one of the best preserved bathhouses on Hadrian's Wall, a well preserved gate, an aqueduct, and a good, traditional museum.

All of the sites are easily accessible off the B6319 that runs west from Heddon-on-the-Wall parallel with the A69. In sections the B6319 runs along the route of the Wall with long sections of the Ditch and *Vallum* clearly visible on either side.

HEXHAM

Hexham is an attractive market town overlooking the River Tyne with narrow streets and lovely parks within easy reach of Hadrian's Wall. It has the Moot Hall – originally a gatehouse of a 12th Century castle and later a medieval court house. There is also the Manor Office, the first purpose-built gaol in Britain (1330) constructed from stone from the Roman Wall, and a grammar school founded in the reign of Elizabeth 1 and established in the existing building in 1684. The market place was built in 1768. The town itself is bustling and attractive, and a pleasure to stroll around. Yet the main reason for a visit is Hexham Priory whose history is chronicled by the Venerable Bede. The Priory began life as a Benedictine monastery dedicated to St Andrew built by St Aidan in the late 7th century from stone taken from the Roman fort at Corbridge. Between 681 and 821 the Priory served as a cathedral when Hexham was a bishopric. The building was largely destroyed by the Vikings in 875 but continued to serve, largely unrestored, as the parish church.

There is speculation that Scotland owes its patron saint to Hexham. It's said that Acca, Bishop of Hexham, was deposed in 732 and took relics of St Andrew – bones from his tomb in Constantinople (Istanbul) – and founded a see on the site of St Andrews in Scotland. This later became the religious capital of Scotland and in 1320 St Andrew was declared to be Scotland's patron saint.

In 1114 the Priory was established by the Augustinian Order. In 1296 it was largely destroyed by rampaging Scots, with only the walls left standing (the Scots were clearly in ill temper during their visit for they also burnt alive 200 scholars in the nearby boys' grammar school). They presumably did a good job in their demolition of the town, for when Robert the Bruce took Hexham a few years later, it was recorded that there was little left to burn. Further damage was done by Scottish raiders between 1320 and 1326. Hexham in these troubled years was not well treated by the Scots who probably wouldn't have acted any differently if they had known they would have it to thank for their patron saint.

The Priory was enlarged in the 14th Century and, after the Dissolution by Henry VIII in 1537, continued to serve as a church. Restoration and embellishment followed thereafter with repairs and alterations still being made to the building in the 19th Century. Its internal architecture is truly superb, especially the 15th Century lofty oak roof of the chancel with its beautifully carved floral bosses.

It has many relics and reminders of its long and interesting history. They include a 1st Century tombstone of a Roman soldier; a wooden rood screen dating from the 16th Century; the 'Frith Stool', once the Bishop's throne and later the seat of sanctuary, carved from a single sandstone block in around 675AD; a font considered to be from the Saxon church; a number of Saxon grave covers; medieval paintings on panels; the shaft of a cross first erected in 740; 15th Century choir stalls and a *lavatorium* dating from the 1300s. However, probably the most moving attraction is the finest Saxon crypt in England, all that remains of the original church. The crypt is built largely from Roman stones, some of which carry pristine Latin inscriptions.

Not all of Hexham's woes are in the very distant past. In 1761 the Riot Act was read in the Market Place outside the Abbey to a crowd opposed to military conscription. The troops panicked after two soldiers were killed, and opened fire on the crowd, killing 45 and wounding 300 more. One ringleader, aged in his seventies, was hanged, drawn and quartered; another, aged eighteen, was sent to slavery in the West Indies.

THE HOLY ISLAND OF LINDISFARNE

Another obvious inclusion on a list of favourite places must be Holy Island, connected to the mainland by a tidal causeway since 1954. Three and half miles long and one mile wide, it's a beautiful place with lovely sea views, some 250 species and subspecies of bird, rolling dunes, mudflats, salt marsh, limestone cliffs, volcanic extrusions and an unspoilt shoreline. There are many distinctive wild flowers, including one, *Epipactis Sanctus*, that is unique to the island.

Also, here are the ruins of an 12th Century Norman priory built, on similar lines to Durham Cathedral, on the site of St Aidan's 7th Century monastery which was destroyed by Danish raiders in 793 and abandoned in 875. Established as a cell of Durham Cathedral in or before 1122, it was staffed by outposted monks from the Cathedral. It was fortified against Scottish raiders in the 14th Century but declined in importance thereafter; it was dissolved in 1537. Nearby is St Mary's Church, built in the 13th Century

but containing some Anglo-Saxon fabric. At the other end of the island on an outcrop of the Great Whin Sill, is Lindisfarne Castle. This was built in 1549 as a defence against the Scots. It fell into disrepair in the 19th Century after it ceased to be garrisoned but came into private ownership in 1902 and was restored extensively inside as a private residence.

However, Holy Island is more to do with atmosphere than buildings. A local historian summed it up as follows: "It is one of the spots in our land which we visit with peculiar feelings of love and reverence, for there did the Christian faith take deep root and become abiding and active". Holy Island has been a place of pilgrimage for 1300 years, and remains so today.

MORPETH

Morpeth, a thriving market town on the River Wansbeck, is the county's administrative centre. More important for our purpose, it has also a number of historic attractions.

The Chantry, the site of the Tourist Information Centre, was built in the 13th Century and for most of its life was a chapel. Also, are the Town Hall first built in 1714 by Vanbrugh and rebuilt in 1870; the Clock Tower built in 1831 of medieval stone; the road bridge over the Wansbeck designed by the famous architect John Dobson and built by the great engineer Thomas Telford; the Church of St Mary, a 14th Century building with later restoration; and Collingwood House, once the home of Admiral Lord Collingwood who commanded the fleet at Trafalgar after Nelson's death.

A little out of the town centre is Morpeth Castle, with its 14th Century gatehouse and 12th and 13th Century curtain walls, all that was left after a Civil War siege in 1644, and the fragmentary remains of a Cistercian abbey founded in 1137. The beautiful Carlise Park is worth a long visit to view its established trees and superb flower beds.

Farther afield – some ten miles west of Morpeth – is Cambo, a model village built in 1740. The village of neat houses and pretty gardens sits around a dolphin-shaped drinking fountain. The post office was once a pele tower. Wallington Hall, built in 1688, contains an historic porcelain collection, a magnificent set of murals depicting Northumbrian historical scenes, and superb plasterwork. The gardens were landscaped by 'Capability' Brown, who was born nearby.

Wallington Hall near Morpeth

NORHAM

On the English-Scottish border overlooking a once strategically important crossing on the River Tweed is Norham, now a delightful village but once regarded as the most dangerous place in England because of its front line position in the Scottish wars. The village has interesting architecture being a blend of painted and natural stone buildings – the former reflecting the Scottish preference and the latter the Northumbrian.

Norham Castle was built by the Bishop of Durham around 1121, initially of timber. It was destroyed by the Scots in 1138, and then rebuilt in 1174 by Henry II. In 1292 Edward I received John Balliol's oath of loyalty here. Four years later war broke out again and the Castle withstood three lengthy sieges (one for a year) but finally fell (briefly) to the Scots in 1327. It also rebuffed a Lancastrian army in 1462 during the Wars of the Roses. After a failed first attempt in 1497, the ill-fated James IV of Scotland finally succeeded in taking Norham in 1513, extensively damaging it with artillery fire. His defeat at Flodden led to the Castle being restored to English hands and a period of repair that continued to 1521. By 1561 it was a ruin, although the 88 foot high keep, still protected by its moat, remains an imposing structure.

In addition to the castle, the church of St Cuthbert is worth a visit. It was built in 1165 on the site of a Saxon monastery founded in 830. In 1202 Edward I met the Scottish earls in the church to arbitrate their claim to the Scottish throne. The church remained basically unchanged until being restored in 1845. Some Norman fabric is still visible.

A short drive from Norham are the villages of Etal and Ford. Etal, a model village, is arguably the prettiest. It has a street of whitewashed, thatched and pantile-roofed cottages that lead to a ford over the River Till. Etal Castle, now a ruin, dates from the 14th Century and was destroyed by James IV in 1497. A chapel next to the castle contains an exhibition on Flodden and the Border Wars. There is also the impressive 18th Century Etal Manor with St Mary's Church in its grounds.

Ford is an estate village built in 1859 by the Marchioness of Waterford as a memorial to her husband. Ford Castle is a good example of a 13th Century fortress and is famous for hosting James IV on the night before Flodden. St Michael and All Saints Church is of the same vintage, though it was restored by John Dobson in 1853. Lady Waterford Hall, once the schoolhouse, is decorated with frescoes of biblical scenes painted by the Marchioness over 21 years.

NEWCASTLE-UPON-TYNE

As said earlier, Newcastle-upon-Tyne (population 260,000) is in the urban south east corner of the region, in the metropolitan county of Tyne and Wear, created in 1974. Although it is therefore strictly speaking no longer part of Northumberland, historically it's a Northumbrian city and it plays an important role as Northumberland's principal shopping, commercial, industrial and entertainment centre. It is easily accessible from most parts of the county by road and rail, and offers all the amenities of a large modern city while remaining a living memorial to its important role in the Industrial Revolution.

Its services and amenities include domestic and international airports, ferry access to Europe and a rail terminus for the rest of Britain. It really is having the best of both worlds for the visitor – there is a big city close by if required, but it's also easily avoided if not.

First founded as a Roman fort and settlement to supply the garrison on the Roman Wall, it became the base for the Norman pacification of Northumberland and is an important link in the defensive fortifications raised against the Scots. The "New Castle" was built of earth and timber in 1080. In 1168 Henry II began rebuilding the castle in stone. It was further strengthened in the 13th Century and additionally protected when Newcastle was enclosed by formidable walls with seven main gates, nineteen towers and many turrets.

The completion of these walls in the 14th Century rendered the castle obsolete, and maintenance appears to have stopped sometime after 1350; by 1589 it was all but a ruin. From the early 17th Century shops and houses were constructed around the site from stone taken from the structures around the keep and the castle walls. Today all that remains are the 82 foot high keep (which once served as a prison), the Black Gate, two postern gates and sections of the old wall – all of which have been subject to protection and restoration since 1809.

Newcastle did have a life apart from warfare. Well before its transformation in the industrial era it was a centre of maritime trade, exporting wool, coal and lead and importing such commodities as iron, furs, corn, wood boards and wine. In the early 14th Century, Newcastle ranked sixth among England's ports engaged in the wool trade; in 1344 it was one of England's wealthiest cities, surpassed only by London, Bristol and York.

Newcastle has an elegant city centre thanks to a major urban renewal project undertaken in the 1830s at the initiative of the builder, John Grainger, to designs by John Dobson and John and Benjamin Green. At its heart is Grey Street, one of finest Regency streets in Britain. This process of renewal continues today with many old parts, such as the quayside, being rebuilt, restored or converted to new uses. The old 'industrial' Newcastle is rapidly acquiring a new future and charm.

Other historic sites include the Guildhall built in 1658; the Cathedral Church of St Nicholas, first built in the 12th Century and gradually rebuilt between the 13th and 15th; the Church of St John the Baptist containing work from the early 12th Century; and Blackfriars, a former monastery dating from the 13th Century. The grand Central Railway Station opened in 1850 was designed by Dobson and covers 17 acres. The Theatre Royal, a fine example of Victorian architecture, is the second home of the Royal Shakespeare Company. To assist visitors to better understand Newcastle's past there are at least ten museums covering such diverse subjects as antiquities, Greek art, archaeology, natural history, pre-Raphaelite art, and motor vehicles.

The city's skyline is dominated by ten railway/road bridges over the Tyne. These include the High Level Bridge, a two-tier bridge built in 1849 by Robert Stephenson; the Swing Bridge built by Armstrong and Company in 1876; the stunning Gateshead Millennium Bridge, the world's only bridge that tilts to allow shipping to pass beneath and the Tyne Bridge, opened in 1928, a miniature of the far more famous (and larger) Bridge over Sydney Harbour in Australia – not surprisingly as they were designed by the same engineering company. There are many other treasures in this large and vibrant city – you just need a little patience to search them out.

ROTHBURY

Rothbury – the capital of Coquetdale – sits on the edge of the Northumberland National Park and is a centre for walkers. The village lies on the north bank of the River Coquet and is surrounded by heather-clad hills. One, Simonside, is famous for its pre-historic sites including burial cairns and carved stones. The village has tremendous charm with its stone houses and shops enclosing a wide main street, and grassy slopes lined with sycamore trees. Dividing the town is the pretty River Coquet.

Rothbury can trace its origins back to the 12th Century, and was granted its market charter in 1291 by King John. All Saints Church dates from 1850 but rests on the remains of a 13th Century predecessor. Below the church is a bridge with a medieval foundation. Cragside House (described above) is just up the road from Rothbury.

WARKWORTH

A short drive south of Alnmouth, Warkworth is a very pretty town dominated to its south by Warkworth Castle. The horseshoe loop of the River Coquet protects three of the castle's sides, with a fortified medieval bridge controlling access from the north. For some three centuries it was one of the most important castles in the north of England and still retains an appearance of feudal power.

A castle was first built on the site in about 1150 by the son of David I of Scotland, who at the time controlled Northumberland. Henry II regained control in 1157 and thereafter substantial re-building occurred creating the structure described in 1249 as a "noble Castle". In 1332 Edward III granted the Castle to Henry de Percy, lord of nearby Alnwick. In the late 14th Century, his successor, then Earl of Northumberland, build the castle's splendid keep. In 1405 Henry IV captured the castle using artillery after the Percy family rebelled against him. Building work was undertaken in the 15th and 16th Centuries, but after 1574 it fell into disrepair. It was wrecked in 1617 and was further despoiled by occupying Parliamentary forces in the 1640s. In 1672 the widow of the 11th Earl of Northumberland sold the castle's structure for building materials leaving the keep a shell. There was some partial restoration in the 19th Century but it was not sustained.

Today all that remains are the ruins of towers (one with fabric dating to 1200), the gatehouse, and sections of curtain wall. However the most imposing of the structures is the three-storey keep described as "one of the rare cases where the military engineer happened to be a great architect". One intriguing feature of this is a light well open to the sky admitting light and air. Rainfall was captured into a large tank and used for cleaning the floors, drains and latrines.

Walkworth's St Lawrence Church is "the finest and most complete Norman church in Northumberland", having replaced a church built by the Saxons in the 8th Century and destroyed by Norse raiders. In 1174, the Scots massacred a hundred or so villagers sheltering in the Church. About half a mile upstream of the Coquet by boat is The Hermitage, a chapel carved out of rock in the 14th Century.

St Lawrence Church, Warkworth

Located a little west of Wooler on the northern edge of the Cheviots is Yeavering Bell, the site of arguably the most impressive hilltop fortification in Northumberland, on a summit 1182 feet above sea level. Built around 400BC it covers some 14 acres and is enclosed by a stone rampart. In the distant past there was a timber amphitheatre, some 130 circular huts and a timber hall 100 feet long. Of these, only the depressions where the huts sat and some internal ditches are evident.

Yeavering Bell was an important tribal base before the Romans came, and continued to be an important military centre for the Gododdin during the Roman occupation. The Old Welsh word *Bryneich*, the name of the early Gododdin kingdom, means 'Land of the Mountain Pass', speculated to refer to Yeavering Bell's commanding position over the valley of the River Glen. Some time after 616AD Edwin, the second king of Northanhymbrie, established his royal palace – an enormous barn-like structure in timber – at a site at the base of Yeavering Bell above the River Glen, known as Ad Gefrin. In 627AD, 3000 Northumbrians were converted to Christianity by St Paulinus at Ad Gefrin. By 670AD the site had been abandoned.

While there is no trace of Ad Gefrin, the hill fort offers an amazing sense of purpose, time and space. The purpose is evidenced by the determination of its inhabitants to build a formidable defensive structure in such an inaccessible place; indeed, there must have been a powerful motivation to do so, suggesting real fears for safety at the time. The sense of time comes from the long period it existed as an operational fort – some 900 years – and its Iron Age origins. The sense of space comes from the feeling of being on top of the world. You can see for miles: north and west into Scotland, east to the North Sea, and south over the Cheviot Hills. The climb is not easy, but most reasonably fit people should be able to climb the footpath to the summit, and the effort is easily worth while.

THE VIRTUE OF FINE GOLF COURSES

W e now turn to the last, and to a golfer the most important, of Northumberland's 'four virtues' – its golf courses. But before describing the courses themselves, it's appropriate to trace the migration of golf from Scotland into Northumberland. Though a game with a few of its modern features may have been played earlier in Holland, Scotland is undoubtedly the home of golf as we know it, being first established there in the early 15th Century. By the end of the 16th Century it was played widely on its east coast. The first golf club, the Honourable Company of Edinburgh Golfers, located at Leith, was founded in 1744. This held the world's first professional golf competition in that year and, to facilitate it, developed the game's first rules – the *Articles and Laws in Playing Golf*. These were updated and expanded first in 1854 and then, more comprehensively, in 1897 by the Society of St Andrews Golfers whose Old Course is the world's oldest continuously used course (since at least 1754).

Golf remained principally a Scottish sport until the second half of the 19th Century; in 1864 there were around thirty golf clubs in Scotland and only three in England. Forty years later the majority of the over two hundred British clubs then in existence were located in England.

Several reasons for the rapid expansion of the game into England have been suggested. The first is the standardization of rules that gave the game the uniform structure required for competition. The second was the growth of internal tourism in England facilitated by its new railway network. To attract custom, many of the seaside resorts built golf courses at which clubs were quickly established. At first these were restricted to sparse land on the coast with little agricultural value and where the grass stayed short naturally. However, the introduction of the grass mower in the 1880s allowed courses to be laid out inland on richer land with luxuriant grass. Finally, there were innovations in golf ball and club design and manufacture that increased the availability and reduced the cost of golf equipment, thereby making it accessible to more people.

Not surprising giving its proximity to Scotland, Northumberland was an early beneficiary of the southward spread of the game. As was the case elsewhere in England after 1864, the first Northumbrian courses were restricted to poorer ground unsuited for agriculture and with short grass. These were the links/seaside courses in Alnmouth Village in 1869; Newbiggin-upon-Sea in 1884; and Dunstanburgh, Walkworth and Berwick-upon-Sea (Goswick) between 1890 and 1896. The last of the seaside courses – Magdalene Fields, Bamburgh, Alnmouth (Foxton Hall), and Seahouses – were laid down in 1903, 1904, 1905 and 1913 respectively.

The two earliest inland parkland courses in Northumberland were built in the 1890s, with a building boom between 1905 and 1913 establishing eight others. With the exception of Ponteland (1928), Prudhoe (1930), and the second nine at Alnmouth, Foxton Hall (1930), the remainder of Northumberland's courses – all inland – were build in the last decades of the 20th Century.

OUR SELECTION CRITERIA

For our review we have chosen the courses we regard as the top twenty in the county. This is not to say that those omitted are not good courses – the truth is that there is not a bad golf course in Northumberland. We should know, we have played them all (often, in most cases). Nevertheless, we felt, given the limited time available to visitors, that it would be helpful to offer them a manageable 'menu' of the more exceptional courses from which they can make their own selection.

We have used three yardsticks for selecting our courses: aesthetics, playability, and hospitality. By aesthetics we mean that they must be visually pleasing. We don't enjoy playing on unattractive courses and we are sure that visitors wouldn't either. In regard to playability we have required that the course must demand a full range of golf shots and intelligent course management, but that it must not be unreasonably hard for higher handicappers. We have taken our lead here from the great player Bobby Jones, who said that a good course is "one that offers equal enjoyment to all standards of player". We have also demanded that at the end of the game we have been able to recall a number of holes that we have regarded as particularly enjoyable to play because of their design or location. A good course should have a number of such holes; if not, its designer has failed. It is holes of this quality that we single out in our descriptions of courses in our reviews.

The last criterion, hospitality, is very important to visitors. A good course will welcome visitors and provide them with at least basic facilities. A great game is no compensation for feeling unwelcome in the clubhouse or pro-shop. Golf is a social game and, as such, courses have a fundamental obligation to receive visitors in the true spirit of fellowship. Also, there should be sufficient access to facilities so that they can have their round in comfort – at least bathrooms and somewhere warm to change. We consider that it is reasonable to expect such facilities to be available whenever the course is open for play, even if the clubhouse is not staffed. We appreciate that many of the smaller clubs are restricted in what they can offer, especially in winter when business is slow. But if the course is open for visitors to play, and pay, it should be able to cater for their basic needs.

None of the courses in Northumberland fails badly in these regards, but we consider that those we have selected for review generally excel in meeting these criteria, or if they have a shortcoming there are strong compensatory reasons for including them

We have grouped the courses we describe into four broad categories: classic links, other seaside, parkland and moorland, although in many cases a course may display characteristics of more than one type. In assigning our labels we have drawn heavily on the typologies in Alan Ferguson's superb book, *Golf in Scotland*.

CLASSIC LINKS

We place these at the top of our list because the links represents a 'pure' golf course, for it was on such courses that the game was born. It's also because they offer a combination of scenery and challenge that is quite distinct to the other course types that might be more familiar to most golfing tourists. Furthermore, those found in Northumberland are exceptional – as good as you might find anywhere in the world. Finally, they are our preferred course type and we feel entitled to be a bit subjective in our presentation. But what is a links course?

The old *Oxford Dictionary* defines them as 'level or undulating sandy ground near a seashore with turf and course grass'. Not all seaside courses are links courses; but to be practical, most run along the coast, and thus a seaside location can be taken to be a useful first defining feature of a links course.

But the essence of a links course is how they evolved. They have, as one writer says, been "provided by the age-long forces of nature". They are a landscape of blown sand created by the wind on the seashore accumulating over the years into dunes and hollows. The golf courses that lie in this environment have been created with minimum interference by man. They look as if an area of natural seascape has been touched lightly to accommodate golf, rather than extensively reconstructed. Designers such as James Braid and Tom Morris simply plotted a route through sand dunes leading away from the clubhouse and then mapped out a path for the return journey using naturally existing features. No earth moving was necessary.

The pure links course is created in the first instance not by machinery or landscapers, but rather by gulls, rabbits, foxes and sheep, all of which fertilised sandy soil and prepared it for later transformation. Man had to do the minimum: to widen the paths made by sheep into fairways, the areas they had closely grazed into greens, and the places they eroded when sheltering from the winds into bunkers. The noted course designer, Sir Guy Campbell, summarised the development of links courses thus: "Nature was their architect, and beast and man her contractors".

Trees and introduced grasses are rare on links courses, as they don't grow naturally by the sea. Apart from limited sheep grazing, links land has little agricultural use, and is barren and desolate in appearance.

With this introduction we now offer these descriptions of Northumberland's six outstanding links courses.

ALNMOUTH VILLAGE

Contact

Phone: (01665) 830370
Mail: Alnmouth Village Golf Club, Marine Road, Alnmouth,
NE66 2RZ.

The Course

Played as 18 holes from the yellow tees, Alnmouth Village is 5654 yards with a par of 70.

Hole	Par	Length	Hole	Par	Length
1	3	199	10	3	199
2	4	322	11	4	322
3	4	295	12	4	295
4	4	360	13	4	360
5	4	269	14	4	269
6	4	290	15	4	290
7	4	362	16	4	362
8	4	430	17	4/5	430
9	4	300	18	4	300

Aesthetics

Almouth Village, opened in 1869, is England's fourth-oldest course (and its oldest nine-hole course). Its designer, Mungo Park, brother of the legendary Willie Park, winner of the first Open Championship in 1860, was a famous golf professional in his own right who won the Open in 1874.

For 60 years what was then the Alnmouth Golf Club shared a course with the Alnmouth Working Men's Golf Club. In 1904 the original course was extended to 18 holes, the new nine created on land owned by the Duke of Northumberland running north of Bracken Hill, a steep ridge evident on the northern side of the course. In 1930 the Alnmouth Golf Club located to this site and built a new 18-hole course incorporating the nine holes built in 1905. This is now Alnmouth Golf Club (Foxton Hall). The Working Men's Club retained the original nine-hole course and clubhouse. In 1935 it was reconstituted as Alnmouth *Village* Golf Club.

Alnmouth Village is a true coastal links running on lean land adjacent to the sea, created with the barest disturbance of the natural terrain. Its fairways are wide and beautifully turfed, drainage is excellent, and the greens are true. From the high point of the course on Bracken Hill there are magnificent views of Alnmouth Bay, miles of beach and dunes, Coquet Island and the pretty Alnmouth village. All holes have the comforting sounds and smell of the nearby sea, though it is this very proximity that gives the course its greatest danger – coastal erosion.

Playability

This was the first course we ever played in Northumberland, on a very cold, windy and wet day that revealed how little we knew about dressing for, and playing in, such conditions. It was very educational, though somewhat humbling as we watched our balls whipped away in all directions by the wind. Playing it again in finer conditions revealed a quite different course. The internal hazards are reasonably benign – principally grass rough and a few shallow bunkers – and competent play gives you a great chance to make or get close to par. Playing 18 or 27 holes here on a fine day is a real treat (your green fee entitles you to a day's play).

The first five holes run parallel to the beach. At the 6th hole, you play up to Bracken Hill; from the 6th fairway and green and 7th tee you have the magnificent views mentioned earlier. There is a steep walk up and down Bracken Hill, otherwise the course is flat.

Four of Alnmouth Village's nine holes warrant special mention. The 4th is a disconcerting hole as it runs alongside a beach with a well-used public footpath; you tend to be conscious of the walkers and their safety and, consequently, to guide the ball to the left into rough. Ahead is a large mound of grass which hides the green. The green on the par 4 5th is slightly downhill and defended by the seashore to the right and rough at the back.

The 6th is Alnmouth's signature hole. Although a short par 4, the drive is blind uphill to a narrow fairway running to the left along Bracken Hill. Even if the shot makes the Hill, there is still plenty of opportunity to find rough or OOB. The green is elevated with steep slopes in all directions to run your ball away. You are now alongside Foxton Hall's 16th hole.

Before hitting off from the tee on the 7th, take in the views from Bracken Hill. Your first shot is over the cliff edge down to a fairway far below. While not a hard shot, it's remarkable how easily you can find trouble with the slightest hook or slice, especially on windy days. Be aware of walkers on the public footpath at the bottom of the cliff.

Hospitality

The clubhouse is open on most summer days from 11am to 3pm with bar and food facilities available except on Tuesdays. Ladies' and gentlemen's locker rooms, and lavatories at the rear of the clubhouse, are both open from 8am until dark. In winter the clubhouse is not regularly open other than on Sundays from 11am until 5.30pm. An honesty box is available when the clubhouse is locked. Alnmouth Village is a bit expensive for a nine-hole course, but the green fee provides for a day's play.

BERWICK-UPON-TWEED (GOSWICK)

Contact

Phone: (01289) 387380 for bookings
Fax: (01289) 387392
e-mail: goswick@btconnect.com
Mail: Berwick-upon-Tweed (Goswick) Golf Club, Goswick, TD15 2RW.

The Course

18 holes, 6467 yards, par 72, played from the yellow tees.

Hole	Par	Length	Hole	Par	Length
1	4	386	10	4	416
2	3	153	11	5	503
3	4	408	12	4	360
4	5	495	13	3	175
5	4	413	14	4	379
6	5	520	15	3	140
7	4	382	16	4	410
8	4	400	17	5	482
9	3	185	18	4	260

Aesthetics

Goswick (*goose dwelling*) was first laid out in 1890 by the great James Braid.
Nine holes were added in 1894 and in 1964 the original nine holes were
modified by Frank Pennick to give extra yardage. In our opinion, it's the
best of Northumberland's links courses.

Braid was five times Open Champion (runner up three times) and an acknowledged world-class course architect. He designed or remodelled over 200 courses in Britain, his most notable works being Gleneagle's *King's* and *Queen's* courses, Carnoustie's *Championship* Course, *Blairgowrie* and *Boat of Garten*. Braid was a 'minimalist' who made creative use of the natural terrain – he simply plotted a route from and to the clubhouse on poor land running alongside the dunes line. Pennick was one of the great modern course designers and Goswick would have been one of his earliest efforts. Among his other works was the redesign of *Royal St George's* to bring it up to a standard to host the Open.

Thus Goswick has an impeccable pedigree and consequently it is not surprising that you find an outstanding links course. It sits in an Area of Outstanding Beauty between the Goswick dunes and farmland (and the main Newcastle to Edinburgh railway line). There are views to the Cheviots, Holy Island, Bamburgh Castle and to the Scottish border hills.

All the features that define a classic links course are found here: sandy soil, fairways running between arable land and the sea with nine running out and the second running back; grass and gorse rough; deep revetted (grass tiered) bunkers, largely treeless, and wind and salt aplenty. Even after heavy rain, Goswick is completely dry underfoot and easily playable. Its greens and fairways are always well maintained.

Goswick is a wonderful course: a classic links with plenty of scenery, variety and challenges. It's a must for all visitors.

Playability

There are no easy holes at Goswick, only some that are less difficult than others. Add a strong wind – a common occurrence here – and you have a challenging round indeed. Even slightly wayward shots will find either

OOB or the thick rough that prevents a clean escape shot – that is, if you can find the ball. Even on a still day expect to lose a ball or two; on a windy day, more.

It's fairly level and thus easy to get round. However, it's a bit rugged – as to be expected from a classic links – and accordingly it's hard to see where the rough ends and the fairway starts. In fact, the direction of the next fairway is not always clear because of the ruggedness of the ground.

Such is the quality of this course, most holes warrant an honourable mention. The 1st, par 4, is a fitting introduction. The fairway doglegs to the right around a stand of small trees and there is a large fairway bunker straight ahead. The first shot has to be well placed to give a clear second shot to the elevated green. At the 2nd, a short par 3, the tee shot is semi-blind over a deep gully and hillock to a fast green sloping to the front. Here you have your first fine view of the coastline south to Holy Island and the countryside west to the Cheviot Hills. From the elevated tee at the 3rd, your shot must clear about 190 yards of rough to reach a narrow section

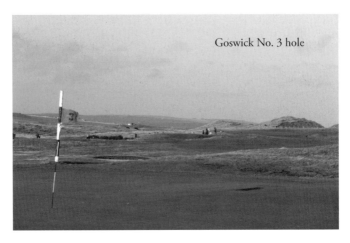

Goswick No. 3 hole

of fairway. There is a temptation to cut the corner to the right but to be successful you would need a straight shot of about 230 yards to clear the rough and fairway bunker. The approach shot is blind to a sloping green marked by a 'barber's' pole.

The recently lengthened 4th is a challenging par 5. It's similar to the 3rd in that the fairway doglegs to the right around an area of rough, again tempting big hitters to cut the corner. To cater for such boldness, there are three hidden bunkers in line 130 to 170 yards out, plus plenty of rough. The pocket handkerchief green is guarded by bunkers and areas of rough to the left and rear. The 5th is Stroke Index (SI) 1, being a long par 4. The narrow fairway doglegs uphill to the left to an elevated green. It plays much longer than its yardage.

There are more lovely views from the 6th, and a lot of work ahead on this long par 5.

Coastal dunes run the length of the fairway to the right (OOB) and the two-tier green is well protected by fairway and flanking bunkers. The fairway at the 7th is narrow with rough on the left and steep slope and rough on the right. The two-tier green has three bunkers on the left, rough on the right, and two fairway bunkers out in front about 20 yards on the left. The 8th is a long par 4 requiring a blind shot to a wide fairway but with a nest of four bunkers straight ahead between tee and green some 200 and 240 yards out on the left. The green is around to the left. The 9th, a long par 3, has OOB in reach on the right and the green is well protected by bunkers.

On the back nine, the 12th, while relatively short, plays much harder than its SI of 8 would suggest. The first shot must be precise to reach a narrow strip of fairway over about 110 yards of rough and three trees. A band of deep rough runs behind the landing area. From the fairway, the approach shot is semi-blind over a gully and rough to the green. The 13th, another long par 3, with its lovely views from the elevated tee, requires a shot down to a heavily bunkered green with a band of trees behind.

Ahead of the 14th tee is a gently curving fairway with three large, strategically located fairway bunkers ahead. The two-tier green is set down in a depression at the base of hillocks. The 15th is a short par 3 but the green is heavily bunkered and has trees at the rear. At the 17th, a long par 5, you hit from an elevated tee, past (with luck) two fairway bunkers. Ahead there are five more well placed fairway bunkers (three across the fairway about 160 yards from the green), a road, and an aggressively bunkered, and sloping, green. The 18th is a fitting finish to a great golf outing. The first shot is from an elevated tee over about a 150 yard stretch of rough and small trees to a narrow fairway. The green is heavily bunkered.

Hospitality

We have considerable affection for Goswick; it's a classic of its type, and is always superbly presented. However, one of its greatest strengths is the warmth of the welcome given to visitors by staff and members.

The clubhouse is attractive and comfortable with full bar services and shower and change facilities for both sexes. Light meals are available every day. The pro-shop is well stocked, does repairs, and has very helpful staff.

DUNSTANBURGH CASTLE

Contact

Phone: (01665) 576572
Fax: (01655) 576562
e-mail: enquiries@dunstanburgh.com
Mail: Dunstanburgh Castle Golf Club, Embleton,
　　　Northumberland, NE66 3XQ

The Course

18 holes, 6039 yards, par 70, as played from the yellow tees.

Hole	Par	Length	Hole	Par	Length
1	4	430	10	4	409
2	4	361	11	4	290
3	4	384	12	4	420
4	3	160	13	3	105
5	4	283	14	5	528
6	4	394	15	3	114
7	4	307	16	4	367
8	4	295	17	4	376
9	4	376	18	4	440

Aesthetics

Dunstanburgh, a classic links course, lies in an Area of Outstanding Natural Beauty on the edge of Embleton Bay on land owned by the National Trust. It was founded in 1900 as a nine-hole course. In 1922 the then owner, Sir Arthur Munro Sutherland, commissioned James Braid to design a new 18 hole course. This was completed in later years to a Braid design with a few further changes in the layout made in the post World War Two years.

Dunstanburgh is long and challenging and has great views over Embleton Bay and beaches, Dunstanburgh Castle and a National Trust bird sanctuary. As to be expected from a classic links course, the soil is sandy and well drained, and the fairways run along and back a narrow coastal strip; they are treeless, have a minimum of manicuring, and are tight and undulating with gullies and dips. Many shots are blind, there are plenty of well-placed fairway bunkers (many revetted), and long grass rough abounds. The wind is often strong and the greens were designed by a sadist. It is a truly great course, and consequently is high on our list of Northumberland's best.

In addition to the other features, you have the sound and smell of the sea, a couple of World War Two pillboxes in the dunes still ready to repel invaders, and a geological curiosity: Saddle Rock, formed by lava intruding between sedimentary layers running into the sea, is visible from the 13th green. The holiday bungalows on the cliff edge at the 4th and 5th holes, with their million pound views, stand smugly ready to provoke your unbridled envy. These date from the 1930s, being erected to house golfers and their families at a time when cars were not generally available.

Playability

It's a toss up between which is harder: Dunstanburgh or Goswick. Dunstanburgh has better defined and wider fairways but its fairways, and at least in the recent past, its greens, are not as well maintained. We will leave it to the visitor to judge.

Notwithstanding, Dunstanburgh, like all classic links courses, has tricks and trials throughout, and a good score is always going to be hard to achieve, especially if the wind gets up. There is one steep climb, from the 1st to the 2nd, but otherwise the course is reasonably flat, albeit a little bumpy to traverse. We can't imagine any golfers, irrespective of their standard, not wanting to play it again and again.

Dunstanburgh 14th hole

The course has some truly fine holes, with the 7th to 9th being what we would describe as examples of 'classic' links holes.

The real adventure begins after you climb a steep hill to the 2nd hole, a short par 4. The fairway doglegs to the left which favours playing your blind, uphill drive to the right with a slope towards thick gorse bushes. To the left is the edge of the cliff and grass rough. However, get the drive right and the rest of the hole is plain sailing. The 3rd has a 90 degree dogleg to the left about 200 yards out. Long hitters can clear the corner with a solid drive but most will be content to follow the fairway. OOB defined by gorse bushes threaten to the left. The green is sloping and protected by large bunkers.

The 4th is a short, but tough, par 3. Before hitting off, look back to the National Trust bird sanctuary and past it to the beach and sea. This will settle you for a 160 yard shot to a plateau green offering plenty of scope for trouble. It is set atop a steep slope and even a good shot could roll off into

77

places that you would rather not be, especially the deep gullies on either side. The tee at the 6th affords wonderful views along the dunes and beach, out to the Bay and across to Dunstanburgh Castle. The drive is from a cliff down to a wide fairway below with bunkers in reach to the left and right. The green is protected by gullies to the front and bunkers.

The 7th is the first of three earlier mentioned 'classic' holes. The drive is blind uphill over a stream to an undulating, narrow fairway framed by tough rough. The approach shot is over a large hollow to a sloping green. The 8th, a short par 4, needs another blind drive, this time along a fairway running parallel to the beach and dunes on the left. A good shot would find a deep gully. The fairway is lumpy with deep dips, and the sloping green is well protected by a gully at the front and by bunkers. To finish the first nine, the 9th is SI 1. The narrow fairway runs parallel with the beach and is undulating and intersected by two difficult-to-avoid deep gullies. The tee shot is blind to a pole. There is another gully in front of the green

Dunstanburgh

The 10th is more scenic than hard: the elevated tee has a beautiful view of the coast and the Castle on the Great Whin Sill. The same applies to the next two holes. At the 12th, there is reachable gorse and grass rough on the right and a turf covered 'wall' across the centre of the fairway. The green is elevated with bunkers on two sides.

The 13th, par 3, is Dunstanburgh's signature hole. You must hit the small green, otherwise the chances are you will be needing a new ball. The shot is 105 yards over a deep gully – to the left is rocky seashore, to the right OOB. This can be an expensive hole on a windy day. Look out to the sea to the left for a good view of Saddle Rock. The Castle almost casts a shadow on the green.

The tee shot on the 16th is straightforward but the placement of the green is cruel. It's tucked away to the right behind a hillock and there are wide bunkers to the rear. Many approach shots would be blind. The green slopes from left to right. The 18th is the longest par 4. There are lines of reachable bunkers along the left and right edges of the fairway and one in front of the green. Avoid these and the approach shot requires those who are not big hitters to make a decision – lay up or go for it.

Hospitality

Visitors are made welcome at Dunstanburgh and are invited to use all the club's facilities. The clubhouse is pleasant and comfortable with a bar and meal service and modern locker rooms for both sexes. It doesn't have a pro-shop, nor does it hire buggies.

Dunstanburgh from the 12th fairway

NEWBIGGIN-BY-THE-SEA

Contact

Phone: (01670) 817344 or 817838
Fax: (01670) 820236
Mail: Newbiggin-by-the-Sea, Northumberland, NE6 46DW

The Course

18 holes, 6190 yards, par 72, played from the yellow tees.

Hole	Par	Length	Hole	Par	Length
1	4	324	10	4	422
2	5	536	11	4	412
3	4	407	12	3	166
4	4	256	13	4	312
5	4	390	14	5	485
6	4	327	15	4	298
7	4	305	16	4	336
8	4	344	17	3	154
9	4	341	18	4	375

Aesthetics

This course came as a real surprise to us. It's a classic links established in 1884 with all the characteristics and virtues of the type, but now in an industrial setting. Dominating the course to the north of the clubhouse are a large aluminium refinery and a power station, but looking back to the south from the 8th to 18th holes you could be forgiven for thinking you are in Scotland. Whatever you do, don't be deterred from playing this gem of a course because of its backdrop – it's simply the legacy of a proud industrial history. In September of 2007 an extraordinary sculpture by Sean Henry, *Couple*, was erected on a platform 250 yards out to sea on the breakwater in the bay; it has two larger than life human forms (they stand about 5m tall), one of either gender, simply standing and staring out to sea. After the game we suggest you visit St Bartholomew's Church, a short way from the clubhouse. The church dates from the 13th and 14th Centuries, and may have earlier origins; it contains over twenty medieval grave slabs. You have a good view of the bay from the car park.

The North Sea is a pervasive presence. It's close by on the right on the 1st to 7th holes, and is visible, or at least audible, on the others. The green on the 3rd can catch the spray from breaking waves if windy.

In addition to the refinery and power station, there are two other tangible reminders of the area's industrial history. There are dozens of horses tethered

around the course, descendants of the pit ponies that once worked underground pulling carts through the mines in the glory days of coal. Also, looking east back along the coast from the 7th tee, you can see smoke venting from an underground mine fire in which coal seams have been smouldering, and may still do so, for decades.

Newbiggin is one of Northumberland's unsung golfing gems, a fine example of a links course that's a credit to its designer(s) and maintenance staff. It's a pleasure to play and we daresay many visitors will want to play it more than once. I know we did even on our first outing when we experienced heavy rain, sleet and bad light, but refused to be deterred from finishing.

81

Playability

This is a difficult course to play well, especially for the first time. Some holes are not easy to follow and there are many testing blind shots over or around difficult terrain. Most of the revetted bunkers are deep, and it's rare not to have at least a stiff breeze to contend with. Nevertheless, with a little familiarity with the layout, even high handicappers should be able to negotiate the course without too much embarrassment. The best chance for a good score rests with the more benign back nine.

There are some very fine holes at Newbiggin. The 3rd is SI 2. The seashore runs along the length of the fairway to the right. The first shot is over an area of rough and a dyke – some 130 yards to the fairway. The green is flanked by bunkers. The 4th is a short par 4 but you have another shot over rough to a fairway protected by a narrow and deep revetted bunker running across its width just where a good first shot might land. The green has bunkers on the left. From this tee, and the next, there are fine views to Coquet Island to the north and to Tynemouth Priory to the south.

The 5th is the first of Newbiggin's great holes. The tee shot is blind over a cove and an area of rough to a narrow fairway – you need to hit about 120 yards to be clear. The cliff edge, and a band of rough, runs along the right side. There is OOB to the left. The second shot is over a pole to a green set down in a hollow. The 6th is another fine hole (indeed our favourite). The tee shot is blind to a pole on a hillock. Ahead is a vast area of rough with a deep gully on the right side. Having cleared the pole about 180 yards out, the small area of fairway doglegs to the right. The slope of the fairway tends to push the ball to the rough on the right or into a deep gully that crosses laterally. The green is set into a hollow at the base of dunes that fortunately encourages roll on to the green (perhaps why the hole is SI 15).

At the 7th the tee shot is again to a pole over 150 yards of rough to the eastern end of the fairway. Big hitters might entertain a direct shot over a mound to get closer to the green but, if short, it could find either rough or two hidden bunkers. The green slopes sharply from the top and left side down to a hollow. From the 8th, the view of the course changes radically. The industrial sites go out of the picture and the landscape ahead is pure links magic. Yet again the shot is over a band of rough, about 120 yards wide, to the fairway. Ahead are three fairway bunkers: one each on either side and, a little ahead of these, one in the middle. The green slopes to the left and is protected by a bunker and an area of rough to the rear. At the 9th the tee shot is blind over rough to a pole 168 yards out. The second shot to an elevated green tucked to the right is also blind, though well marked by a pole.

The back nine is, in our opinion, the easiest half of the course and the holes are somewhat less interesting. The 12th is a par 3 (166 yards). Of this distance 100 yards is over rough and a dyke. The green has bunkers to the left and right. At the 13th the shot from an elevated tee must clear 130 yards of rough and a ditch to reach the fairway. There is a dyke about 40 yards in front of the green. The 15th is a short par 4. The green is close to the green on the 3rd and can have the backdrop of breaking waves. Three fairway bunkers sit out about 200 yards to two sides.

Hospitality

The clubhouse is very comfortable and well appointed inside with full facilities for both sexes, but there is no pro-shop. Members and greenkeeping staff are rightly proud of their course and happy to give you its history, and tips on how to play it well.

SEAHOUSES

Contact

Phone: (01665) 720794
Fax: (01665) 721994
Mail: Seahouses Golf Club, Beadnell Road, Seahouses, NE68 7XT

The Course

18 holes, 5169 yards, par 67, played from the yellow tees.

Hole	Par	Length	Hole	Par	Length
1	3	131	10	3	126
2	5	440	11	4	362
3	3	171	12	4	417
4	4	349	13	4	270
5	4	401	14	3	180
6	3	145	15	3	109
7	4	372	16	4	305
8	4	316	17	4	372
9	4	369	18	4	348

Aethestics

We play here regularly with John and Marjorie Chilton and have come to regard the course, the staff and members as old friends. But this is not why we have included it – it deserves its inclusion on its own merits, being an old links course (1913) that offers interesting golf, and a couple of memorable holes, without being physically tiring. The views from the course are magnificent – inland to the Cheviot Hills, along the coast to the north are the Scottish border hills, Holy Island, and Seahouses harbour, while to the south are the wide sands of Beadnell Bay with Dunstanburgh Castle in the distance. Out to sea lie the Farne Islands. Seahouses has two of the most renowned par 3s in Northumberland, the 10th over a large pond and the 15th over a sea cove.

The fairways are undulating with large tracts of rough to catch your ball. Ten holes have OOB close, and the greens are slippery. Four of the greens (8th, 9th, 11th and 18th) have two tiers; a design feature credited to Alister Mackenzie who for two decades before 1934 designed some 400 courses, including some of the world's finest, including *Augusta*. We suspect that Seahouses must be one of the first of Northumberland's courses to reflect this design feature.

It is a compact course and the 4th/7th and 9th/18th holes share wide fairways. It's necessary to be aware of other golfers when playing these holes. Care must be taken when crossing the busy coastal road from the 2nd green to the 3rd tee and back again from the 8th green to the 9th tee. There are also popular public footpaths which cross parts of the course, especially along the coast.

Seahouses is another of Northumberland's fine links courses. It will test and please golfers of all standards and some holes are truly memorable. The views are exceptional, the fairways dry underfoot, and the greens immaculate and hard to read. This is a wonderful course by any definition.

Playability

Seahouses is a reasonably short course and generally forgiving. However, the rough is long and there are some really testing holes. This, combined with a low par, makes it challenging even without its difficulty being amplified by windy conditions. The older holes on the sea side of the road are particularly intimidating.

It has some great holes. The par 3 1st kickstarts your round with its lumps and bumps to a green with well-placed bunkers. The 2nd is Seahouses' only par 5. To have any chance of making par the drive should carry an area of grass rough and humps about 180 yards ahead of the tee. At the outer end of this area a high ridge across the fairway acts as a natural 'fence' to catch the ball. The green has a small stand of trees on the left and water close by at the back. At the 3rd there is a stream to the left that intrudes into the side of the fairway. (Note the lovely old stone bridge to the left of the tee, once part of a main road, now bypassed). The 5th, a strong par 4, is SI 1. A drain and fence (OOB) on the right runs the full length of the fairway and to the left is a row of trees in play for the drive. Straight ahead and running towards the left is a watercourse.

At the 8th a new stand of trees forms a wide OOB band that intrudes into the fairway from the left. Also on the left is a fairway bunker. The small green is slightly elevated, and is well bunkered. There is a stand of trees to the right. The 9th hole has three hidden bunkers on the left side of the fairway and there is grass rough on the right. The fairway is undulating and the roll to the green is blocked by a ridge across the fairway. A bunker is incorporated in the left side of the ridge. The green has bunkers on both sides and is on two levels.

The 10th, par 3, is the club's signature hole – the famous *Logan's Loch*. The shot is taken from an elevated tee across a water-filled former (limestone) quarry to a smallish green perched on the edge. This is a memorable hole, to be enjoyed whatever the fate of your tee shot. Before hitting off at the 11th, take time to enjoy the lovely views along the coast to the south. The drive is blind uphill to a pole on an elevated fairway. A line of bunkers across the fairway protects the front of a two-tier green. The 12th is the longest par 4 and SI 2. There are fabulous views from this tee to the Farne Islands, Seahouses harbour, and coastal cliffs (and their seabirds). The drive is blind to a post. Walking towards the green enjoy the views towards the Cheviot Hills. The green is set below the level of the fairway and guarded by two bunkers across its front. At the 13th a stone wall (OOB) runs along the left-hand side of the fairway. Watch out for the bunkers on the right-hand side. The green is elevated and well protected on both sides by bunkers and the OOB on the left. Be alert for walkers on the coastal path who can suddenly appear just behind the green.

Seahouses: 14th Green looking south towards Dunstanburgh

The views for the 14th tee are the same as those from the 12th. It's a long par 3 with the cliff edge running along the left side of the fairway; the green is only about 20 yards from the cliff edge. Again, watch out for walkers. There is a nesting colony of kittiwakes on the cliff next to the tee.

The 15th is another fine par 3. It requires a shot 120 yards from one side of a cliff to another over a sea cove. As with the 10th, a very precise and positive shot is required. Most average golfers will be unnerved by this hole, but it's one to enjoy. The 16th is another intimidating hole; the drive is blind over about 100 yards of rough to a narrow fairway with rough on the left. The second shot is to a downhill green perched precariously above the 10th green. An extravagant shot could put you in the water below the 10th green.

Seahouses, 15th hole

The beach and dunes (OOB) run along the left side of the 17th fairway for its full length, and to the right is an elevated area of rough. The green is tucked to the left and has water to the rear and left and is on two levels. The 18th takes you back to the clubhouse. The main road runs to the left alongside the undulating fairway for its full length. There are fairway bunkers on the left and the two-tier green is protected by a formidable array of bunkers. The folk in the clubhouse are well placed to enjoy your finish.

Hospitality

Seahouses is one of the friendliest clubs imaginable. It appreciates visitors and makes them most welcome. For this reason, however, it can be very busy. In addition to the many Club competitions it holds, especially at weekends and during the summer months, many visiting groups have Seahouses on their itinerary. The clubhouse is very comfortable, with all facilities for both sexes, and provides meals and snacks.

WARKWORTH

Contact

Phone: (016655) 711596.
Mail: Warkworth Golf Club, The Links, Warkworth, NE65 OSW

The Course

Nine holes, 2909 yards, par 35. The course may be played using alternate tees for a second nine. However, the difference is only marginal, with the second nine only 215 yards shorter at 2694 yards, par 35. Visitors play from the club's back tees.

Hole	Par	Length	Hole	Par	Length
1	3	211	10	3	212
2	4	375	11	4	393
3	4	290	12	4	323
4	4	294	13	4	379
5	5	441	14	5	435
6	3	173	15	3	246
7	4	278	16	4	293
8	4	288	17	4	324
9	4	344	18	4	304

Aesthetics

This classic links course was designed by the great golf architect Tom Morris and was opened in 1891.

Morris is one of the greatest names in golf – indeed he is regarded as the father of 'minimalist' links design as reflected in the works of later designers such as James Braid. Morris won the Open Championship four times, the last in 1867 at the age of 46. His works include Prestwick and the original design of Muirfield, and he made extensive modifications to the Old Course after being appointed Custodian in 1867. As to be expected from a Morris design, Warkworth has all the features found at the other links courses in this book: located between sea and farmland, minimum disturbance to natural features, sandy soil, treeless, open and exposed, salty and very windy. It offers superb views of Alnmouth Bay, Coquet Island and Warkworth Castle, and is a great walk even without the golf, which would please Mark Twain.

Tom Morris
1821-1908

At this point it is timely to describe an unusual feature of many Northumbrian courses, including Warkworth's 6th and 9th fairways. These are distinctive, corrugated, land patterns called riggs – parallel ridges and furrows running along or across fairways. These are a consequence of a land use in which the same furrows were ploughed continually over hundreds of years to create high-backed ridges on either side on which the crops were planted. It was common in medieval times, reaching its zenith in 1350, and in some areas followed ploughing patterns originating before the Roman conquest of Britain. The system persisted in many parts of Britain – probably including Northumberland – for several centuries, in some places to the mid 19th Century. The patterns exist wherever land has escaped extensive cross-ploughing in modern times, and the areas preserved in Northumberland's golf courses are among the best examples found in Britain.

While only a nine-hole course, Warkworth will test you, and besides you can always do it again from the alternate tees for added pleasure. The golf is great, especially the first five holes, and the views even better. Apart from two holes, the course is flat and easy to walk.

Playability

As was the case with Alnmouth Village, we first played here on a very windy day and had the devil's own job staying on the fairway. We lost count of the balls carried seaward. Later games in calmer conditions were more agreeable. It's really not a hard course – the fairways are mostly wide, the hazards are not overly penalizing, and the greens are true.

The 1st is a long par 3 where the first shot is downhill from an elevated tee. There is a steep walk down from the green. The 2nd is SI 2 and the longest par 4. This hole runs along the lower level of the course within a band of dunes and seashore on the right. The fairway is undulating with bunkers on the left (two) and right (one). The green is set down behind a hillock and slopes left; there is rough to the right.

We have great memories of the 3rd where you must hit a precise blind uphill shot to the fairway if the heavy rough on the hillside is to be avoided. The green slopes to the front and OOB is close to the right. The fairly narrow fairway on the 4th runs along the edge of the cliff (to the right). OOB is a constant risk, especially in a wind. The green is protected by six well-placed bunkers, the cliff edge and a steep gully behind. The alternate tee position adds 80 yards and makes the 13th hole SI 1.

The 5th is also along the cliff edge and your first shot must clear a deep gully. The green slopes to the right. This gully comes into play again on the 7th, and a fence is OOB on the right. The green slopes to the right and is protected by three bunkers in front. OOB is in easy reach on two sides from the tee at the 9th. Fairway bunkers guard the approach to the bunker-flanked green.

Hospitality

Visitors are welcome except on Tuesday and Saturday. The clubhouse is basic but comfortable and offers bar facilities. While a locker room is available for men when the clubhouse is shut, there is none for ladies – an unfortunate omission. An honesty box operates if the clubhouse is shut. Our only other concern is that it's a bit expensive for nine holes – even such historic nine holes – but your green fees entitle you to a day's play, so it's not too bad.

OTHER SEASIDE COURSES

As we said earlier, not all seaside courses are links and those now described, while having some links characteristics, fail to meet the full complement of qualities that define links. All describe themselves as "coastal" or "seaside" and while such generic terms suffice as a shorthand, they fail to do justice to what are three extremely interesting, attractive and challenging courses.

BAMBURGH CASTLE

Contact

Phone: (01668) 214378
Fax: (01668) 214607
e-mail: bamburghcastle@hotmail.com
Mail: Bamburgh Castle Golf Club, 40 The Wynding, Bamburgh, NE69 7DE

The Course

18 holes, 5241 yards, par 68, played from the yellow tees.

Hole	Par	Length	Hole	Par	Length
1	3	180	10	3	188
2	3	209	11	4	324
3	5	422	12	4	421
4	5	474	13	4	407
5	4	307	14	3	162
6	3	208	15	4	383
7	4	273	16	4	261
8	3	121	17	4	238
9	4	355	18	4	308

Aesthetics

We are fortunate that our great friend, Adrian Herd, is a proud member of Bamburgh. His generosity in taking us as his guests to Bamburgh has allowed us to play it more often than we might have been able to do otherwise. Nevertheless, before we met Adrian, we had played Bamburgh several times and already concluded that it was our favourite of the Northumbrian courses. Playing it more frequently has only confirmed this assessment.

This stunning course was designed by George Rochester, whose other works include Alnwick and Morpeth, and was laid out in 1904. It starts on the cliff edge overlooking the sea, but soon runs inland to elevated land, so it has a pleasing mixture of links and moorland characteristics. In any event, it's one of the most beautiful and interesting courses imaginable. If physical beauty were the sole criterion, Bamburgh would be among the very best golf courses in Britain.

The course wends its way around and through an area of high land rising from the coastal plain and has magnificent views of the beaches running north and south, Budle Bay, the craggy citadel of Bamburgh Castle, Holy Island, the Farne Islands and open farmland. The sea is visible at every hole. It's hard to imagine a golf course anywhere with a better suite of views. The AA *Guide to Golf Courses* summed it up well: "for sheer breath-taking beauty [it] cannot be bettered".

The terrain of the course – gullies, rocky outcrops, elevated tees and greens, punishing rough, and natural hazards of gorse and heather – add to Bamburgh's distinctiveness. However, in among this natural jumble the fairways and greens are immaculate.

Playability

The course is not long but almost every hole is a test of accuracy and character. It would be a rare visitor who could expect a par round. Many first and second shots are blind, and it's a course that must be approached boldly. Just take what comes and enjoy it, especially if the wind is up, and don't fret if you lose a ball or two. We guarantee you will remember this course for a long time.

It should be said that Bamburgh is a physical course, requiring a bit of an uphill slog for about 75 per cent of the way. That said, it seems to pose no problems to its more elderly members – probably because they appreciate how fortunate they are to play on such a sublime course.

Almost every one of Bamburgh's holes is memorable, the 1st being no exception. This longish par 3 (180 yards) requires a drive to a green set on the edge of a cliff running along the fairway on the right side. Not one for those of us bedeviled with a slice. The 2nd is no problem, but the 3rd, a short par 5, certainly is. The first two shots (at least) are blind uphill to a fairway with a natural slope to the right towards rough. The green is tucked away to the left. The 6th, the aptly named "Plateau", is SI 1. It's a long par 3 at 208 yards, especially as the green is steeply uphill. The tee shot has to be a beauty to make the grade; a short shot could see the ball roll back down the hill.

The 8th is a short par 3 at 121 yards, but pinpoint accuracy is required. The small bowl green is over a wide/deep gully and is protected on the right by a rocky spur, and on the left by a bunker. Over hitting will find rough at the back. To finish the first nine, you have a par 4 with an elevated tee looking down to wide fairway below (and Budle Bay). There is no real problem with the tee shot (wind allowing) but the second shot is blind to a downhill green with an impossible amount of trouble all around.

The 10th, a long 188 yard par 3, is also from an elevated tee. The tee shot is blind to a pole over an area of gorse and rough ground stretching out about 150 yards. Remember to ring the bell when the green is clear. At the 11th, it's a blind uphill shot to a post over a gully with heather and gorse in close play. From the top of the hill there is a dogleg to the left. A road sits close behind the green. From the tee at the 12th you have the view of Holy Island depicted in the painting by Russell Flint hanging in the clubhouse. At 421 yards this is the longest par 4. The fairway runs parallel to a road on the left. The drive is blind uphill to a post and the second shot is downhill to the green. There are trees and rough at the rear of the green.

An uphill fairway at the 13th, par 4, makes this 407 yard hole play a lot longer (and thus SI 2). From an elevated tee you look out over 120 yards or so of gorse rough. The first shot is downhill and the second is blind uphill to a post. The green is protected by a stone wall and bunker on the right, a bunker on the left, and rough at the back. The 14th, a par 3, is a truly formidable hole: you hit uphill over a gully to a semi-hidden, elevated green protected by gorse and rough all round. There is very little clear landing area apart from the green and it's unexceptional to lose your ball.

Bamburgh Castle
from the
14th green

At the 15th tee you are at the highest point of the course so take time to enjoy a panorama that includes the Castle, Budle Bay, beaches, Lindisfarne and the Farne Islands. You start a downhill run from the 15th. Your shot is blind to a pole set against the backdrop of Budle Bay and a long view north towards Scotland. The second shot is also downhill and must clear a deep gully in front of the green. Leave your bag and trolley at the top of the steps and take your putter and driver with you (you come back this way on the next hole and by this time you will want to save your energy).

The 16th, a short par 4, requires a blind shot over the deep gully, then a second shot along a narrow fairway that doglegs left. There is hillside heather on two sides. Don't over club as you will lose your ball if it goes through the green. The castle provides a wonderful backdrop to the green as you come along the fairway. The 17th would be a horror hole in the wind; even in the best conditions it offers plenty of trouble. The drive is from an elevated tee through a narrow passage with farmland (OOB) on the right and a hillside of rough on the left. The gentlest hook or slice will get you into trouble.

Hospitality

This is one of the most exclusive and expensive courses in Northumberland, but it accepts visitors without hesitation, and offers them all of its facilities. The clubhouse is charming, comfortable and complete, offering locker rooms with showers for both sexes and full bar and meal facilities. There are restrictions on visitors playing on weekends, holidays and competition days. There are a limited number of buggies for hire but these must be booked in advance. As to the cost – forget it. Bamburgh is simply too fine a course to quibble over pennies.

ALNMOUTH – FOXTON HALL

Contact

Phone: (01665) 830231
Fax: (01665) 830922
e-mail: secretary@alnmouthgolfclub.com
Mail: Alnmouth Foxton Hall Golf Club, NE66 3BE

The Course

18 holes, 6007 yards, par 69, played from the yellow tees.

Hole	Par	Length	Hole	Par	Length
1	4	411	10	4	413
2	4	380	11	3	140
3	4	432	12	4	313
4	4	421	13	4	462
5	3	163	14	4	340
6	4	414	15	4	306
7	4	324	16	5	482
8	3	121	17	3	190
9	4	324	18	4	361

Aesthetics

At this stage an interest must be declared – John is a member of Foxton Hall and has been for some years. This arose from a casual encounter with a couple of members in the clubhouse after we had completed a round on a wet and windy winter's day. They were intrigued by our dedication, or stupidity, and appreciative of our genuine admiration for the course. One thing led to another, the invitation to seek membership was issued, and the deed was done.

We have already mentioned Foxton's orgins, its having been established in 1930 on land made available by the Duke of Northumberland and incorporating nine holes from the then Alnmouth Golf Club (now Alnmouth Village). Its design is the work of Harry Colt, the first amateur golfer to earn an international reputation as a golf architect. Colt was one of the first architects to take the game inland and in so doing developed skills in drainage, soil preparation, strategic bunkering and tree planting. Other courses he either designed or remodelled include *Muirfield, Hoylake, Portrush, Royal Lytham and St Annes, Sunningdale (New Course),* and St Andrew's *Eden Course*. He is credited with the idea of the 'double loop' – taking the 9th and 18th holes back to the clubhouse.

Foxton's fairways, greens and grounds are superbly maintained and, consequently, the course is always immaculate. Colt's hand is evident in its clever layout, fertile soil, effective drainage, and its 'double loop' layout – indeed, it is probably one of the first English courses to bring you back to the clubhouse at the 9th hole.

In addition to its fine fairways and greens, and its well-placed trees and shrubs, Foxton Hall offers lovely coastal and rural views from most holes. The front nine is well treed and has a couple of holes running along the cliff top overlooking Alnmouth Bay and Foxton Beach. The back nine is more open and largely treeless with grass rough providing the more common hazard. The sea is in almost constant view throughout the course.

Sections of the course have old riggs and furrows that give the fairway a corrugated appearance. There are also well-preserved World War Two pillboxes on the 2nd, 6th and 15th holes.

Playability

Foxton Hall will appeal to players of all standards. There are enough benign holes to help an average golfer to a reasonable score, but there are also some that will test the best, especially in the strong wind to be expected from a coastal location. Six of the 13 par 4s are over 400 yards, about half the holes require at least one blind shot, some two, and the bunkers are situated to punish both bad, and unlucky good, shots. The course is largely flat with only the 14th and 15th holes requiring a climb.

Foxton Hall doesn't have any what might be described as truly spectacular holes. Rather, its impact comes from the generality of its good holes, of which nine warrant particular mention.

The 2nd is along a fairway that slopes to the left towards OOB with the direct route to the blind green blocked by fairway bunkers and a stand of trees. The 3rd is SI 1 and the second longest par 4 at 432 yards. Ahead from the tee is a deep gully (with water) while there are reachable bunkers on the left (two) and right (three) contracting the landing area. More fairway bunkers lie ahead of the green to test the approach shot. The 5th is arguably the best of Foxton's par 3s. Before hitting off, take time to admire the wonderful views from the tee. You are directly over the beach and have long coastal views to the south. The green is 163 yards out, slightly downhill and well protected by bunkers. The cliff edge (OOB) is on the left. The long, par 4, 6th requires a blind drive to a pole over a deep, heavily vegetated gully. Fairway bunkers to the left and right are reachable, but are well to the sides. The cliff edge (OOB) runs along the fairway to the left.

The back nine starts easily enough with two gentle holes (though the 10th is a long par 4), but the 12th is more difficult; this is a short par 4 but you have a blind drive out to a post, with three well-placed fairway bunkers on the right and grass rough on the left. The approach shot is also blind down a steep slope to a green marked by a tall post. Remember to ring the bell when the green is clear. The 13th is the longest par 4 at 462 yards. From the lower level adjacent to the 12th green you drive up a steep slope to a fairway running to the right towards the sea. The most direct route to the green is uphill over two deep fairway bunkers set into the slope. Thereafter it's a long haul towards the sea with more fairway bunkers ahead.

At the 14th, the drive is blind up a steep slope that can run your ball downhill towards a band of trees and well out of sight of the green. The fairway is narrow with a slope on the left side also. Our next destination is the 15th green, and the highest point of the course with superb views in all directions. This is reached by a blind shot along a steeply uphill fairway with trees and a fairway bunker on the left blocking a direct line to the green. To finish, the 18th is not particularly hard but offers the prospect of some embarrassment for poor play; the green is under the clubhouse windows, and in full view of armchair critics.

Hospitality

Foxton Hall has the reputation in local golfing circles of being an exclusive course – a reputation perhaps enhanced by its history and charming old clubhouse. While it is no doubt a club with high standards, we have always found that visitors have been welcomed with courtesy. The clubhouse amenities, including its mixed bar (serving meals), a snooker room, television lounge, bar meals, and modern change/shower facilities for both sexes, are available for the use of visitors.

Accommodation is available in the Club's Dormy House (eight twin-bedded rooms and two single rooms).

MAGDALENE FIELDS

Contact

Phone: (01289) 306120
Fax: (01289) 306384
e-mail: mfgc@firefly.clubd24.co.uk
Mail: Magdalene Fields Golf Club, Berwick upon Tweed, TD15 INE

The Course

18 holes, 6235 yards, par 72, played from the yellow tees.

Hole	Par	Length	Hole	Par	Length
1	4	285	10	5	500
2	4	338	11	4	380
3	5	515	12	4	352
4	4	355	13	4	300
5	4	370	14	3	206
6	4	408	15	5	500
7	4	360	16	4	368
8	3	160	17	4	292
9	4	396	18	3	150

Aesthetics

Magdalene Fields is the most northerly golf club in England and is further north than many Scottish golf courses including the Open Championship venues of *Turnberry* and *Troon*. It was established in 1903 and was designed by Willie Park, twice Open champion and one-time Professional at *Musselburgh*. With Harry Colt, Park was one of the first of the designers to sculpt their courses rather than simply make use of existing features. After creating a host of courses in Britain, including the *Sunningdale Old Course*, he spent most of his life between 1916 until his death in 1925 in the USA.

Most holes run alongside, from, or to a coastal cliff above the North Sea and several offer panoramic views north to Scotland and south to Berwick-upon-Tweed and Holy Island. All holes are exposed to the wind; a critical factor in how the course plays on any given day. The fairways are open and lush and several have deep riggs and furrows blunting the run of the ball, and the greens are immaculate and true.

The course has another asset – its historic setting. It runs to the side of the walls of Berwick's Elizabethan fortifications (a dry moat is a hazard on two holes), and some remains of the Norman wall are also visible. This backdrop, together with the seaside views, makes Magdalene Fields one of Northumberland's most scenic courses.

Playability

The course is testing and on a windy day is a real handful. However, the pars for the holes are fair and the fairways are wide enough to give confidence to those who wish to hit out. It's flat but there is a bit of a walk between some greens and tees.

Magdalene Fields has a number of fine holes. The 3rd is the longest par 5. The fairway heads to the sea in a sweeping dogleg to the right with three fairway bunkers on the right. The first and second shots are blind to poles, and the green has three bunkers on the right, and is set downhill and close to the cliff edge. There are lovely coastal views from the green. The 6th is the longest par 4 with a fairway that takes a soft dogleg to the left. The green is slightly elevated and sloping.

The 7th is one of the course's best holes. The fairway doglegs downhill and heads to the sea. The green is precariously placed on the cliff edge and well protected by bunkers on both sides. Overshooting is a real danger here, with a lost ball the consequence. There is a slope to the right of the green that will carry a ball into a steep gully, and perhaps over the cliff. The 8th, the aptly named 'Good Luck', is Magdalene Fields' signature hole. While a short par 3 at 160 yards, you hit to the green from one side of a cliff to another over a sea cove. The green is protected by the cliff edge to the right, and two bunkers on two sides. Pray for a still day. Before hitting off, enjoy the superb long views of the Scottish coastal cliffs to the north, the coastline below, and over Berwick and Holy Island to the south. The 9th, a strong par 4, is SI 1. OOB runs to the right along the length of the uphill fairway. The sloping green sits close to the OOB and the railway line to the rear – there are bunkers left and right.

The 12th is called 'Humps' for good reason. There are riggs and furrows running left to right across the fairway, blunting the run of the ball and giving you either uphill or downhill lies.

Riggs and furrows (humps) on Magdalene

There are good views here of Berwick's Elizabethan walls as well as a section of its original Norman wall. At the 13th, you drive over the dry castle moat towards a slightly downhill fairway. The danger here is a wayward shot to the right that will find the bowling club buildings and OOB. The green slopes slightly to the left and has bunkers on two sides. The drive on the 15th is downhill to a pole. Thereafter the fairway sweeps to the right. The green has two bunkers on the left. Enjoy the panoramic views of Berwick and its harbour and the coastline to the south.

The 16th is ominously – and aptly – named 'Destroyer' (SI 2). The tee is set downhill on a cliff edge from which you have good views of the coastline to the south, Berwick-upon-Tweed, and the beach below. The drive is blind over a cliff face to a pole some 80 yards ahead. When on the fairway be careful to keep away from the cliff edge on the right which runs along most of the fairway. The fairway at the 17th takes a sharp turn to the left about 150 yards out. You are tempted with your second shot to cut the corner and hit directly to the green over an area of grass rough. **A warning:** the designer anticipated such boldness by placing three concealed fairway bunkers just ahead of the green on this line. Be bold – it's more fun.

To finish, you have a memorable par 3. This hole requires a shot from an elevated tee to a small green set 150 yards on the right edge of the castle moat and well protected by bunkers. The more timid can play to the right, but if you seek par, go for it.

Hospitality

Magdalene Fields makes visitors most welcome, and the clubhouse is comfortable and offers all the facilities a visitor might require including a bar service between 11am and 11pm every day including meals (limited on Tuesdays). It's somewhat irritating that the ladies' and men's changing rooms (in a separate block, next to the car park) are kept locked, but they will be opened on request by bar staff. There is a limited pro-shop in the clubhouse. There are buggies for hire.

PARKLAND COURSES

The majority of Northumbrian courses fall into this category. In their purest form, parkland courses are fully man-made, constructed to prevail over the natural terrain, not to blend unobtrusively into it. Their soil is rich and retains moisture, and is thus able to support large trees and shrubs; their hazards are strategically inserted rather than naturally occurring. Water hazards are introduced through lakes and ponds – generally receptacles for drainage run-off. Trees are often used to define fairways and to act as hazards, and the rough is principally long grass. They are typically manicured and ordered.

However, while still evidently the outcome of deliberate design, the parkland courses of Northumberland are not all of the highly manicured variety typical of the breed, for two reasons. The first is that the growing conditions – with the harder winters – impose restrictions on the vegetation and grass that can be grown. To increase the playing season, greenkeepers have kept to the natural landscape, grass and other vegetation of the area that cope best with the weather rather than introduce more exotic, and visually more pleasing, plantings.

The other reason is that many local parkland courses are built over clay – in some cases over reclaimed opencast coal mines. Accordingly, tree growth is slow so it's unusual here to find large trees in profusion except where they run through very old woodland (as is the case for example with *DeVere Slaley Hall*, *Arcot Hall*, *Hexham*, and *Stocksfield*). Because of the clay base, drainage is often inadequate to clear heavy rain. While fairways are well mown and lush, greenkeepers here tend to leave longer rough and to spread it around more generously. Another exception is that there are not the large water hazards associated with many parkland courses, though *Longhirst Hall* stands apart in this regard.

This notwithstanding, the parkland courses of Northumberland are lovely places with challenging designs. Moreover, they have managed to avoid the common fault with such courses of a boring layout with parallel fairways separated by trees. Each has its own style and character that offer unlimited variety to the visitor.

ALNWICK

Contact

Phone: (01665) 602632
e-mail: mail@alnwickgc.co.uk
Mail: Alnwick Golf Club, Swansfield Park, Alnwick, NE66 1XN

The Course

18 holes, 6101 yards, par 70, played from yellow tees.

Hole	Par	Length	Hole	Par	Length
1	4	359	10	4	324
2	3	136	11	4	381
3	4	403	12	5	565
4	3	155	13	4	370
5	5	510	14	4	292
6	4	357	15	3	159
7	4	436	16	4	341
8	4	409	17	3	171
9	4	362	18	4	371

Aesthetics

Alnwick is one of Northumberland's best parkland courses, with panoramic views out to sea in the distance. It was first established in 1907 with nine holes designed by George Rochester. The land on which it sits was once part of the grounds of Swansfield House, the mid 19th Century residence of HC Selby, the Duke of Northumberland's Steward.

The original nine holes were extended to 18 holes in 1995, the new holes occupying land on more open countryside. The new section of the course between the 5th to 15th holes runs along the eastern edge of the Northumberland hills and provides wonderful views over the coastal plain to the sea some five miles away. The course has good drainage, fabulous fairways and excellent greens.

On the way to the 17th tee admire the weathered Camphill Monument, a 19th Century column erected by HC Selby to commemorate the end of the Napoleonic Wars. The mounded area under the 16th green is the site of a pre-Roman British camp. Low-flying fighter jets on training flights often provide a more modern, and startling, distraction.

Playability

Alnwick plays like two discrete courses. The original holes are tight and require accuracy to avoid the mature trees and bunkers, but on the new section you can really open your shoulders because the fairways are wide and mostly treeless. However, the rough is hard to avoid, and escape, and you must watch the fairway slope and the well-placed bunkers.

All holes are challenging, and the wind can be a problem on the more exposed section. The greens run true but don't let you off lightly. One hole, the 3rd, is very steep and could tax the less mobile. The 2nd, 12th and the 14th to the 16th also require a bit of a climb.

Golfers must be aware of walkers on the two public footpaths crossing the course – they have right of way.

Alnwick has many excellent holes, and a couple that are memorable. The 2nd, par 3, is only 136 yards but difficult to play well if you are unfamiliar with its layout. Your shot is blind uphill to a green protected by trees on two sides. The green slopes downhill and is hard to read. The 3rd is a 403 yard par 4, and justifiably SI 1. The drive is blind up a steeply sloping fairway with mature trees closing in on both sides. Most golfers would be content to reach a narrow level area about half way up. This gives you a position from which to make the top, but again the shot is blind. Thankfully, once on the upper level it's an easy iron to the green. Take time to get your breath back before proceeding.

The 5th is the start of the new section of the course. It's a strong par 5 at 510 yards. You drive from an elevated tee to a wide fairway with an old quarry to the left and heavy grass rough to the right. From here there are fine views across the coastal plain to the North Sea. The 7th is the longest par 4 (436 yards). There is a slight dogleg to the left with a hedge constricting the fairway at its middle. A fence (OOB) runs along the right side of the fairway. The elevated green has two tiers. At the 9th the green is set to the right reached by either continuing along the fairway or more directly across a corner of grass rough. There is a steep slope to the right of the green which is further protected by trees at the rear and a bunker.

View over 9th green to the sea

At the 11th, the drive is from a tee tucked close to the old quarry. There are fairway bunkers in reach on the left and right, and the shot to the green has to contend with hawthorn trees in front. Then you come to what many regard as Alnwick's hardest hole (despite it being SI 2), the 12th, par 5. The drive is to a fairway that doglegs to the left with the quarry on the left side, a hawthorn tree and two bunkers directly ahead on the fairway, and a large area of gorse to the right. Thereafter, it's uphill to an elevated green. The 13th is another fine hole. The drive is over a fence downhill towards a green tucked downhill and to the right behind a large area of gorse. Thereafter you have a choice: add a stroke by approaching the green along the fairway or take a chance on a lost ball and shoot blind over the gorse.

At the 15th you return to the 'original' holes. This is the longest par 3 and slightly uphill. Your shot must clear gorse stretching about 100 yards in front to reach a green protected by bunkers. At the 16th, par 4, the first shot is blind uphill between a gap in a wall and two large trees. Don't go right as large trees can block the approach to the green. Thereafter, the shot is to a raised green protected on two sides by trees and a slope in front. You have arrived at the Camphill Monument and at the green you are standing on an ancient site. The finishing hole is blind uphill to a fairway sloping steeply to the right and OOB; then steeply downhill. OOB is in easy reach on the right side. The green slopes steeply to the right towards trees and OOB.

Hospitality

No problem here – Alnwick is a most welcoming club. The existing clubhouse is a bit basic, but is warm and friendly with all necessary facilities, including drinks and bar meals. A new clubhouse is in prospect and this will improve the facilities for members and guests alike. A small number of buggies are available for hire in summer.

ARCOT HALL

Contact

Phone: (0191) 2362147
Fax: (0191) 2170370
Mail: Dudley, Cramlington, Northumberland, NE23 7QP

The Course

18 holes, 6097 yards, par 70, played from the yellow tees.

Aesthetics

Hole	Par	Length	Hole	Par	Length
1	4	320	10	5	506
2	3	159	11	3	185
3	4	364	12	4	452
4	3	200	13	4	348
5	4	388	14	4	376
6	5	505	15	3	148
7	5	498	16	4	412
8	4	363	17	4	328
9	3	173	18	4	372

Arcot Hall was a surprise to us. We hadn't heard it mentioned by those with whom we have discussed local courses, so we went fearful that we might be disappointed. In the event, we found the opposite: a very attractive, exacting and mature parkland course that warrants greater recognition in local golfing circles.

The Club was founded in 1909 as the Benton Park Golf Club on another course designed by James Braid. In 1948 it moved to its current location, previously the property of the National Coal Board (the ground under the 1st, 17th and 18th holes was an opencast mine, but there is no evidence of this now). The Club changed its name to Arcot Hall in 1958, adopting the name of the manor house in whose grounds the course runs. The Hall was built in 1803 and named after the fortified town near Madras where Clive of India won distinction in 1751.

The course has an interesting design: nine holes form an inner circle with nine around the perimeter. It's well wooded and there are pleasant walks between greens through areas of trees and shrubs with the occasional sightings of rare red squirrels and other wildlife. There is an enchanting feeling of rural tranquillity.

Typical of parkland courses would be to find it wet underfoot after rain, but we have played here without discomfort when other courses were closed. After we had played Arcot Hall we hit upon a possible reason why we had heard so little about it: the members want to keep this gem to themselves.

1st Hole at Arcot Hall

Playability

The course demands both distance and accuracy, but is reasonably forgiving for all standards. The fairways are generally wide, encouraging big hitting, but many tee shots are out of narrow tree-lined alleys; many holes dogleg, some sharply; the sloping greens are well protected by bunkers. Most fairways are corrugated by riggs and furrows that hinder fairway run.

Let's look at some particularly fine holes. At the 3rd, the first shot on this reasonably long par 4 is over a stand of small trees; there is a small pond hidden on the right. The deeply rigged fairway veers right and narrows as you approach a sloping green well protected by bunkers and trees. At the par 5, 6th your drive is out from a narrow alley framed by large trees. A small watercourse sits to the left about 200 yards out. The fairway narrows as you approach the green. The sloping green is protected by a fairway bunker 50 yards out in front to the right and flanking bunkers. The next hole is the shortest par 5 at 498 yards. The fairway is heavily rigged and has reachable bunkers on the right and left. The green is sloping, has trees close by on the left and rear, and a bunker on the right.

The 8th is a real tester for those of us unable to work the ball reliably. A reasonable length, but the drive is through a tight gap and the fairway doglegs sharply to the right around a stand of timber. The approach shot has to contend with a large fairway bunker stretching across the middle. The sloping green has trees to the rear and a bunker on the left. You finish the opening nine with a pretty but challenging par 3. The first shot is 173 yards to a smallish sloping green that has a pond hidden to its left. There are trees and shrubs on two sides, a bunker to the left and another out in front.

The 15th, 'Saunders' Rest', is a short (148 yards) par 3, that challenges because of the trees impinging on the drive and a pond to the left. It has a poignant, charm for here rest the ashes of Lt Commander Saunders RN who served his Club as Secretary for many years and won its enduring respect and affection. He was clearly a towering figure in the Club's proud history.

At the 16th, par 4, the fairway doglegs to the left around a band of mature trees. A strong drive is needed to allow a clear approach shot. The two-tier green is tucked into the right corner with a large bunker on the left, and another on the right, and trees to the rear and right.

The final holes are other examples of where Arcot Hall demands the ability to work the ball. The 17th doglegs sharply to the right and is bordered on both sides by mature trees. The green is downhill, slopes in two directions, and has bunkers on two sides and trees close to the right. At the last hole, the fairway turns sharply to the right around a band of large trees (OOB) and the tee shot is through a 'window' framed by the band and a large tree on the left. The sloping green is set back close to the front of the pro-shop, has trees on the left and a large tree out in front to the right, and bunkers on both sides. This is a truly fitting end to a very enjoyable round.

Hospitality

The clubhouse is very comfortable as you would expect from a renovated former manor house. But there is no pretension here; the reception is warm and we were impressed with the obvious pride that its members and staff have in their course. Full access is given to the elegant clubhouse which has all the facilities a visitor would want. The pro-shop is fully equipped and its staff very helpful. Restrictions apply on weekends, but even then a game is possible.

DEVERE SLALEY HALL

Contact

Phone: (01434) 673154
Fax: (01434) 673152
e-mail: slaley.hall@devere-hotels.com
Mail: De Vere Slaley Hall Golf Resort and Spa, Slaley, NE47 OBY

The Courses

Hunting: 18 holes, 6530 yards, par 72, played from yellow tees.
Priestman: 18 holes, 6271 yards, par 72, played from yellow tees.

Aesthetics

These two magnificent parkland courses are set in 1000 acres attached to the Slaley Hall Hotel, a former grand Edwardian country retreat converted into a luxury hotel and resort. Hunting, a European Tour venue, is the older course (by a decade). It was designed by Dave Thomas, a former champion golfer and runner-up in the 1958 Open Championship.

However, despite Hunting's tournament recognition, both courses are of similar length and standing, and offer spectacular golf. The fairways traverse testing and picturesque terrain with mature trees (including very old oaks), areas of gorse and grass rough, banks of rhododendron and other flowering bushes, deep and plentiful bunkers, and huge greens, often two-tiered and never easy. Many of the greens are 'blind' from the tee for at least the first shot. The fairways are superbly grassed and water is a feature on many of the holes, adding both to the visual appeal of the courses and to their difficulty.

An added complication is the prevailing and often strong westerly wind that the locals say is funneled through the Tyne Valley between the North Pennines and the Cheviots. The courses sit on top of moorland and are exposed to the wind and weather, so fairways facing west typically play much longer than their length. They are physical courses, climbing up and through hilly countryside, so older players may prefer to use the buggies available for hire.

We have no hesitation in recommending both as 'must play' courses – they are among Northumberland's very best.

Hunting

Hole	Par	Length	Hole	Par	Length
1	4	399	10	4	338
2	4	390	11	5	529
3	4	392	12	5	490
4	5	483	13	4	362
5	4	332	14	3	156
6	3	186	15	4	315
7	4	409	16	4	350
8	4	373	17	3	159
9	4	431	18	4	436

Playability

This is really two courses in one. The first nine is fairly level, runs through woodland, has particularly tight fairways and water is in play on seven of the holes. On the plus side these holes are better protected from the wind. The second nine runs up, down and along open west-facing countryside and, while more forgiving, is open to the wind. The fairways are wide with few trees and with water on only three holes.

This is not a course on which all but the best golfers could expect to get a low score – there is too much scope for inaccurate play to wreck the card. After all, it's a true championship course. However, if this is accepted in advance, the compensation is a superb course full of interest and excitement. Low handicappers would revel in what it offers.

As these comments suggest, there is an abundance of fine holes here. At the 2nd, the green, and for that matter the direction of the fairway, is hidden from the tee. However, a good drive of around 200 yards to a fairly small landing area will reveal all. Watch out for the bunkers ahead and the watercourse to the right. The fairway takes a sharp turn to the right and the second shot, assuming a good drive, is across the watercourse to an elevated green guarded by two bunkers (one an 'island' bunker) in direct line. There is another first blind shot at the 3rd. This must clear a watercourse and the landing area is very tight. There is a large bunker on the right about 170 yards out. The large green has two tiers and flanking bunkers. The 5th is the easiest hole on the front nine but good fun nonetheless. The only danger from the tee is a bunker to the right about 180 yards out. But the green has three levels, a lake and watercourse to the left, and two bunkers on the right.

The 6th is a long par 3 at 186 yards over a large lake – you must hit 150 yards to clear the water. Even if you do this, there is a watercourse and large bunker to the right of the green. The more timid golfer can lay up to the right of the lake, but why miss the fun? Straight ahead at the 7th at about 180 yards, you have a lake to the left and two large trees to the right. From these the fairway runs uphill to a two-tier green protected by flanking bunkers (the one on the left very deep) and banks of rhododendron on two sides. The green at the 8th is hidden as the fairway doglegs to the right. Ahead of the tee is an area of rough about 120 yards out and the small target area has watercourses in front and to the right. The second shot is downhill and must clear a watercourse running across the fairway 70 yards out from the green. The green is elevated with flanking bunkers.

The 9th is Hunting's signature hole – and SI 1. The fairway is uphill and flanked by large pines. A watercourse runs along the left side and across the fairway about 150 yards in front of the green continuing along the full length of the fairway on the right. The green is elevated and has two tiers. There is a large bunker to the left and a smaller one to the right.

The back nine is more open to the wind and relatively free of trees. The 11th is a long par 5. It's straightforward for the first shot, but the next shot(s), must contend with a stream and a band of rough about 170 yards out from the green. The two-tiered green is uphill, narrow and well protected by bunkers. The 13th is a short par 4 at 362 yards but has a gully with watercourse 210 yards ahead. As the fairway is downhill it's easy to run your ball into trouble. The second shot is to an elevated green tucked to the left with the usual flanking bunkers. The 14th, par 3, requires a strong shot uphill through an avenue of pine trees. The green has two levels and large bunkers providing protection. The fairway on the 16th is framed by trees on both sides and doglegs to the left. Three fairway bunkers sit to the right at the corner in the 160 to 220 yard range.

The 18th is described by the course as "one of the hardest finishing holes in golf" and we won't disagree. The first shot is blind and steeply downhill towards a ravine and watercourse 270 yards from the tee. A good drive could see the ball run into trouble. Because of a large stand of trees on the right, you must stay on the left side to have a clear shot to the green. The shot to the elevated and sharply sloping green is over three bunkers along the left side of the fairway.

Priestman

Hole	Par	Length		Hole	Par	Length
1	4	350		10	5	521
2	4	337		11	3	132
3	3	154		12	4	382
4	5	481		13	4	377
5	3	157		14	4	384
6	4	355		15	3	147
7	4	393		16	5	464
8	5	474		17	4	410
9	4	360		18	4	393

Playability

Priestman, like Hunting's back nine, is more open with fewer trees. However, it runs through more challenging terrain and has water in play for over half of its holes. Perhaps this would be easier than Hunting for higher handicappers, but only marginally. Like any championship course it is not designed to be kind, so again accept whatever comes with good humour and enjoy being on such a fine course.

Let's look at some of its best holes. The 2nd is a short par 4 at 337 yards but requires considerable precision to negotiate. The fairway doglegs to the right and the drive must reach 200 yards to have a clear shot to the green. Otherwise, you have trees at the corner blocking your path. The green is protected by two bunkers – the two on the right are large. At the 4th, you start with a blind shot downhill to a marker pole. The second shot is played from a down slope and must clear 220 to 250 yards over a large fairway bunker to the left and two lakes, one straight ahead and the other to the left of the green. It's prudent to lay up here. The two-tier green is protected by large bunkers on the right and the lake on the left.

The 5th is a reasonable par 3 (157 yards) with a lake to the left of the fairway and two large bunkers to the right. The fairway slopes to the lake. The 7th is a long par 4 (393 yards) and SI 2 for both ladies and men. The first shot is downhill to a generous fairway. However, thereafter the fairway winds to the right around a lake which remains in play right to the green. The green is narrow and sloping and protected by two large bunkers. The fairway on the 8th is slightly uphill and split by a nest of three bunkers about 100 yards in front of the green. The two-tier green is set to the right protected in front by a large oak and a bunker.

The 10th is Priestman's longest par 5. The first shot is towards a nest of five bunkers some 200 yards out from the tee, and the second has to cut the corner of the dogleg but fall short of a second nest of bunkers on the left side of the fairway. The third shot risks a pond and watercourse running across in front of the green. The green has two levels and is further guarded by a band of trees on the right and flanking bunkers. The 11th, par 3, is played downhill over a blind ravine and watercourse. The green has a large bunker to the right and four others to the left and rear. On the 14th, the drive is over a ravine with trees to the left and a line of three bunkers directly ahead. Thereafter, the fairway doglegs to the left with trees intruding at the corner. There is another ravine about 100 yards out from the green. The two-tier green is guarded by the usual complement of bunkers.

The 15th is a memorable par 3. The shot is to an elevated green with a ravine and watercourse in front and a bank of gorse bushes close by to the left. The green has three large bunkers, one to the left front and two to the right. While the 16th is a short par 5, the fairway is uphill and has a watercourse running across and along the right hand side. Further ahead – 145 yards out from the green – the fairway is split by two large bunkers. The plateau green has three bunkers on the left and gorse and trees to the right. The 18th is another great finishing hole. The drive is blind downhill across a watercourse with a large bunker running along the right side of the fairway. The green is protected in front by large trees on both sides and a lake to the front left. The green has three levels and bunkers in front and at the rear.

Hospitality

I suppose it has to be said that the reception here is more correct than intimate, but this is to be expected given the size of the operation and the large number of visitors that play the two courses. That said, we have no complaints about the professional way we have been treated by the staff, both in the pro-shop and in the hotel.

The facilities for golfers are superb. The changing rooms are elegant and the snacks and meals are excellent. The pro-shop is stocked with all that a golfer might need (though catering for the upper end of the income scale). Buggies are available for hire and there is a driving range if you wish to practise. Tee times are 10 minutes apart ensuring a good break between groups. If you need accommodation the hotel is very luxurious and offers full resort facilities including a swimming pool, gym and health spa. The original grand home has been preserved with modern wings added.

HEXHAM

Contact

Phone: (01434) 603072
Fax: (01434) 601865
e-mail: info@hexhamgolf.co.uk
Mail: Spital Park, Hexham, Northumberland, NE46 3RZ

The Course

18 holes, 6000 yards, par 70, as played from yellow tees.

Hole	Par	Length	Hole	Par	Length
1	5	480	10	3	178
2	3	160	11	5	481
3	4	383	12	4	392
4	3	166	13	3	131
5	4	365	14	4	400
6	4	436	15	5	480
7	4	357	16	3	109
8	4	420	17	4	383
9	4	340	18	4	339

Aesthetics

The introduction to Hexham is impressive: down a pretty, tree lined road and then into the grounds of a former manorial estate. Even before you leave your car, you suspect that you are in store for a golfing treat. You are not wrong.

The Club was founded in 1889 and moved to its current site in 1907. The course was designed by the great Harry Vardon and Jack Caird, then the Professional at the City of Newcastle Golf Club. Vardon, the populariser of the eponymous grip, won the US Open and six Open Championships. He, James Braid and HS Taylor formed the 'Great Triumvirate' that dominated golf for 20 years after the 1890s. By 1905, Vardon had a host of courses to his credit. In regard to Hexham, he wrote that he was impressed by "the beautiful nature of the turf" and that "for scenery it can hardly be surpassed". In 1920 James Braid designed the bunkers that were added to increase the course's difficulty.

In 1951 the Club purchased Spital House and its grounds (143 acres). The house, which was built in 1802 on the site of a hospice for lepers founded in 1114, was converted to a clubhouse in 1955. The course is historic, elegant and beautiful, set in hilly parkland and framed by magnificent old trees including oak, beech, conifers, ash and birch, augmented by new plantings. The old trees provide a superb backdrop and constant hazards, while the hilly course offers fine views of the Tyne Valley. The fairways are well drained and nicely grassed, but slope sharply in places; the bunkers are large, deep and cleverly placed; the greens are immaculate and fair.

One of the oak trees, near the 5th tee, is said to be over 400 years old. According to legend the townspeople of Hexham left food under a tree on the same site for the lepers at the nearby hospice. In November 2000 an acorn from the old tree was planted next to the 5th tee which has now grown into a healthy young tree. The *AA Guide to Golf Courses* says that Hexham is "as good a parkland course as any in the north of England". We agree without reservation.

Playability

This is a superb course but it is hard to play well: it's hilly, and requires good course management and accuracy to avoid the trees and to avoid problems from the sloping fairways. There is a good mix of hole lengths and while most are relatively short for their par, any advantage is negated by their elevation or testing configuration. We have played well enough here, but still had ordinary scores. But who cares when playing a course this good?

The opening hole sets the scene for a great golf outing. The drive is downhill to a fairway set at the base of a ridge and edged on two sides by large trees. It needs to be over 200 yards to give a clear shot to the green as the fairway doglegs to the left. The second shot is downhill and the third up to an elevated green protected by two bunkers. The 2nd is arguably the most testing and prettiest par 3 on the course. The shot is 160 yards uphill to a green with a steep drop to the right to two large bunkers and plenty of trees around. At the 3rd, the drive is downhill to a fairway that doglegs to the left with a bunker to the right at about 210 yards. The second shot is uphill to a plateau green with a large bunker on the right.

The 6th, a par 4, is SI 1 because of its length and uphill run. The fairway doglegs to the left and the landing area for the drive slopes towards an area of tough rough. The green has flanking bunkers and a slope to the rear right. The views from the tee of the countryside and River Tyne are stunning. The 7th starts with a blind first shot that must avoid trees and OOB on the right. From the top of the hill the second shot is downhill to a green protected by two bunkers. The 9th requires an uphill shot with danger from a string of fairway bunkers to the right. The green is tucked into the hill on the left and protected by a deep bunker 20 yards out on the right, flanking grass banks, rough and trees on the right.

At the 10th, the shot is over a valley to a plateau green 178 yards out protected by a large oak on the right and a bunker to the left front. The 11th is the longest par 5 with your drive blind uphill to a flat fairway guarded by a bunker to the right. A further bunker sits on the left of the fairway to catch a loose second shot. The green has a bunker out to the front and another on its left. The 12th is a longish par 4 with an uphill first shot, thus SI 2. The two-tier green is flanked by bunkers. At the 14th, the fairway doglegs slightly to the left with large trees on that side. There is a fairway bunker 60 yards out from the green to the right, and the green has three bunkers and OOB on the right.

At the par 5, 15th the fairway doglegs to the left with OOB close to the right. The green is protected by two bunkers and rough at the rear. The 16th is a short par 3 with danger from a large tree to the left of the tee, and, at the green, two large bunkers and trees to the right. There are two options at the 17th. The safer of these is along the heavily treed fairway that doglegs to the right, while a more dangerous route is between a narrow corridor of trees direct to the green. You would have to be very good – or optimistic – to attempt the latter. But the safe route is no pushover: you need a drive of over 200 yards to have a clear shot to the green. The 18th takes you back to the clubhouse. You drive off a high tee down to the fairway, and then hit your second to a sloping green protected by three bunkers, rough at the rear, and OOB on the left

Hospitality

The staff and members of Hexham are rightly proud of their course and are pleased to help you enjoy it fully. However, there are restrictions on visitor play at weekends. The Georgian clubhouse is grand and comfortable and offers full facilities including change rooms/showers and bar, restaurant meals and snooker room. The separate pro-shop is well stocked.

LINDEN HALL

Contact

Phone: (01670) 500011
Fax: (01670) 500001
e-mail: golf@lindenhall.co.uk
Mail: Linden Hall Golf Club, Longhorsley, Northumberland, NE65 8XF

The Course

18 holes, 6117 yards, par 72, as played from the yellow tees.

Hole	Par	Length	Hole	Par	Length
1	4	382	10	4	382
2	4	358	11	4	368
3	5	516	12	4	357
4	3	136	13	5	534
5	4	366	14	4	363
6	4	373	15	3	144
7	3	123	16	5	463
8	4	266	17	3	142
9	5	487	18	4	357

Aesthetics

Linden Hall is a wonderful course designed by Jonathan Gaunt, and while we are unaware of his other design work he has our admiration for this creation. It offers a roller-coaster ride through mature woodland, moorland and lovely parkland. It's one of our favourite courses and we strongly recommend it to visitors.

The course is long and testing and runs through both mature woodland and open parkland. Large trees run through and around the course (the old oaks are particularly splendid), there are fine long views over beautiful farmland, the Cheviot Hills and the North Sea, the four par 3s are memorable, the greens are immaculate and slippery and creative use is made of ponds and streams for hazards on ten of the 18 holes. In addition, there are large bunkers located to do maximum damage to your score. The fairways are not pristine and some areas might be wet underfoot after rain.

On the front nine there are heavy banks of rhododendron. The birdlife, including geese, pheasants, ducks and swans, are welcome company. There is a feeling on the course of playing 'at home' in the grounds of the lord's manor with glimpses of Linden Hall Hotel, once a grand manor house, to which you return at the 9th and 18th. At its front is a ha-ha, a walled embankment that restrains livestock without affecting the view from the house.

Linden Hall doesn't take itself seriously as the friendly epigrams on signs dotted around the course attest, such as, *You're only here for a short visit. Don't hurry, don't worry and be sure to smell the roses along the way* (Walter Hagen) and *I'm hitting the woods just great but I'm having trouble hitting out of them* (Harry Tascana). A great mixture of beauty, design, challenge and fun.

Playability

This is not an easy course, and high handicappers will struggle to write a good card. But any golfer who is content to be challenged will enjoy playing it. It has hidden dangers and traps for those playing it for the first time, and most holes place a high premium on accuracy. The course is largely flat, but there are long walks between holes (buggies are available for hire).

There are many excellent holes, and a good number that are truly memorable. The 2nd is one of the shorter par 4s but is rich with danger. There is a pond to the left of the fairway in the 160 to 220 yard range and a large fairway bunker on the other side. For really big hitters there is a stream crossing the fairway 260 yards out from the tee. The green is undulating with a large bunker on the right. The 3rd, a par 5, plays all of its 516 yards. The first two shots are blind uphill with fairway bunkers within reach of both on two sides. About 60 yards out from the green the fairway turns right at a point marked by a large tree and bunker on the right with a stand of mature trees on the left; these narrow the approach to the green. There are lovely country and sea views from here.

Then you find the 4th, the first of Linden Hall's superb par 3s. This is a breathtaking hole. The elevated tee looks down to a small green 136 yards out with a large pond in front and to the left. Added protection is given by a large tree to the right front and mature trees close by the rear of the green. There is no safe option – hit the green, or lose your ball more than likely.

At the 5th, the drive is downhill to a fairway with a gentle right-hand dogleg. There are two fairway bunkers on the left and a large lake to the right. The green is undulating and bunkered on three sides. The 7th is the second

Linden Hall 7th green

of the memorable par 3s. This is short but the downhill green has a large pond lying close to the left and mature trees rear and to the right. The green slopes to the left towards the pond. This hole is a little more forgiving than

131

the 4th due to the small area of space on the right, but not by much.

The 8th is the easiest hole on the course, so why do so many of us find it so hard? The fairway is slightly uphill, narrow and banked on both sides with bunkers on the left and right. The sloping green has two bunkers on the right and one on the left. You come back to the imposing Linden Hall Hotel on the 9th. The drive is from an elevated tee over a gully towards fairway bunkers on the left and right. A large pond intrudes into the left side of the fairway about 150 yards out, to the surprise of those who don't know the course. The green is bunkered front left and right.

The 10th is SI 1, a good length par 4. The drive is uphill to a fairway that doglegs to the right. Fairway bunkers sit on the left and right (two). The two-tier green has a bunker about 30 yards to the front on the right, another to its left, and trees at the rear. The 13th is the longest par 5. The first two shots are blind. The drive is along a narrow tree-lined fairway towards a pole 250 yards out with fairway bunkers on both sides. The fairway then turns left for about 150 yards then resumes its original course for the final 140 yards. At this point the right side of the corner is obscured by a large tree. The green is guarded by a pond to the left and a water course running in front and to the right.

The 15th is the third of the memorable par 3s. The green is 144 yards over

a lake and there are mature trees on both sides to catch those scared of water. Missing the green may not lose your ball – but you would need some luck. The 16th is a short par 5 but runs uphill.

Fairway bunkers (four) run relentlessly along the left side of the fairway to the green to discourage corner-cutting. The sloping green has bunkers on two sides. The 17th, the last par 3, is the least breathtaking of the four, but a fine hole nevertheless. The shot is 144 yards downhill over a stream to a green with a lake on the left and rear and two bunkers on the right.

You return to the hall via a great finishing hole. There is constant danger from lakes along the right side of the fairway. The green is obscured on the right by a large stand of trees. A pond sits to its left and in front is a gully with stream. There are also flanking bunkers. Threading a needle thoughts come to mind here. Walking back to the pro shop, admire Linden Hall and its ha-ha.

Hospitality

Linden Hall is geared to visitors, whether from off the street or from the Hotel, but you must contact the pro-shop in advance. There is no clubhouse as such as the bar and meal facilities are provided by the Linden County Pub located just across from the well equipped pro-shop. However, there is an excellent change/toilet/shower facility next to the pro-shop. There is also a driving and chipping range.

LONGHIRST HALL

Contact

Phone: (01670) 791509
Fax: (01670) 791385
e-mail: enquiries@longhirstgolf.co.uk
Mail: Longhirst Hall, Longhirst, Morpeth, NE61 3LL

The Course

Championship Course, 18 holes, 5643 yards, par 70, from yellow tees.

Hole	Par	Length	Hole	Par	Length
1	4	329	10	3	146
2	4	384	11	4	271
3	5	447	12	4	336
4	4	363	13	4	272
5	3	166	14	3	153
6	3	130	15	3	185
7	4	370	16	5	496
8	4	390	17	4	368
9	4	299	18	5	538

Aesthetics

We went to Longhirst on the recommendation of friends who are keen birdwatchers and loved the birdlife found there. However, they failed to mention that the birdlife was there because of the extensive lakes, ponds and streams in play on most holes.

The original 'Florida-style' parkland 18-hole course, built on the site of a former opencast coal mine, was opened in 1997. Extra holes were added in 2003 to form two courses, the *Championship* and the *Leisure*. The *Championship Course* uses 6 holes from the original plus 12 new holes but it would be impossible for a visitor to distinguish the new holes from the old. The fairways are immaculate, though they can be boggy after rain.

The *Championship Course* has its best days still ahead as its many small trees mature and add to its attractiveness, variety and difficulty. The water hazards distinguish it from other Northumberland's courses – by both their abundance and location. Of the course's 200 or so acres, over 20 per cent is under water. True to the Florida inspiration, the large greens satisfy USGA specifications and most have considerable slope and wave-like undulations that make them hard to hold and read.

From the higher ground, there are fine long views over the Northumberland coastal plain. The rich variety of birdlife, including swans, geese, ducks and water hens, is a bonus for those who enjoy such pleasures.

Playability

The ten par 4s are reasonably short and there are five par 3s, so a reasonable score might be expected. But don't count on it; Longhirst offers a considerable challenge. The heavy rough around the course and the placement of the water hazards will test most golfers to the maximum, especially when played for the first time because some hazards are not readily visible.

The course is flat, but there is a fair walk from some greens to tees so we suggest that less mobile players hire one of the plentiful buggies available.

Most of the holes warrant mention in this review because of their design and use of water. The 2nd is a strong par 4 (SI 2). From the tee there is water to the left and a fairway bunker to the right. A good drive sets you up for a second shot to the green over water crossing the fairway in front of the green, but if it falls short laying up may be the best option. The green is elevated, slopes back towards the fairway, and is protected by a large bunker on the left. The 3rd is the only par 5 on the front nine. A solid wayward drive to the right from the elevated tee will find a lake, as might a misdirected second shot. There is water running across the fairway in front of the elevated and sloping green. Ahead at the 4th are two vast lakes that run almost continuously along the left side of the fairway and behind the green. OOB run close along the right side for about half the fairway's length. The green is undulating.

The 6th is a superb par 3. The shot is from an elevated tee to a green almost completely encircled with water. The green slopes to the left towards the water. Pinpoint accuracy is a must if the green is to be held. The 7th is a good length par 4. Lakes on the left and right are intimidating but not a real menace. However, the large, undulating green is tucked to the right with a large (hidden) pond directly in front. Water is in play from tee to green on the 8th, the longest par 4. The drive is to a pole and must skirt a lake on the right. The second shot risks a lake on the left side and a pond with trees and rough to the left side of the green. The green slopes downhill to the fairway and is undulating. The first shot at the 9th is over a lake to a pole about 150 yards out. There are lakes on both sides of the fairway running to the slightly raised green. As usual this has slope and undulations.

At the 10th, the shot is to the sloping green from an elevated tee over the corner of a lake on the left. A second lake sits on the other side of the fairway. The 11th, a short par 4, has a lake ahead of the tee. To be clear of danger the drive must be at least 170 yards. The undulating green slopes back to the fairway. The 12th doglegs to the right with a lake on the left side. From about 200 yards in front of the green, the fairway slopes towards the water. A second pond sits close to the left side of the elevated and sloping green. From the 13th tee the drive is over the corner of a large lake to reach a fairway that doglegs to the left. The undulating green has a lake to the right and rear. While it is difficult, we were surprised that this 272 yard, par 4 hole is SI 1.

The 15th is the longest par 3, downhill over water to a sloping green. The slightly uphill fairway at the 16th seems much longer than its 496 yards. It doglegs to the left with a fairway bunker hugging the curve. The 17th is Longhirst's signature hole, and a beauty. From an elevated tee you have reachable water to the left. The second shot is to a green tucked to the left over a stream with lakes on either side. Small ponds protect both sides of the green. There is no room for error.

Hospitality

Reception is in the clubhouse, some distance from the starter's box. We have found the welcome at reception polite and proper, but not particularly warm. We suppose this is because it's a business rather than a golf club so there is a different attitude. However, visitors have full access to the clubhouse which is open every day and has a bar (with meals available), full locker facilities for both sexes, and a pro-shop.

There is a hotel, Longhirst Hall, nearby (with 75 en suite bedrooms) as well as self-catering accommodation. The resort offers extensive facilities such as gym, tennis, sauna and spa.

We have one complaint. In winter you may be asked to play off small mats on the fairway. Fair enough, but as these allow the course to stay open in conditions that might otherwise see it closed, these should be made available free (with deposit returned on their safe return). We suggest that any visitor asked to buy a mat refuse and go to one of the other courses available within a short distance.

MATFEN HALL

Contact

Phone: (01661) 886400
Fax: (01661) 886055
e-mail: info@matfen.com
Mail: Maften Hall Golf Club, Matfen, Northumberland, NE20 ORH

The Course

18 holes 6355 yards, par 72, played from yellow tees.

Hole	Par	Length	Hole	Par	Length
1	5	462	10	3	130
2	4	284	11	4	336
3	4	380	12	4	440
4	4	437	13	5	479
5	3	182	14	4	434
6	5	488	15	4	366
7	4	344	16	5	491
8	3	164	17	3	193
9	4	423	18	4	322

Note

Since our review, Matfen has added a new nine-hole course which will in time join the existing 18 holes (now designated as separate courses) as a 27-hole complex. The intention is to give guests the option of playing different combinations of the three nines.

Aesthetics

Maften is a mature and rather splendid parkland course set in the spacious grounds of the Matfen Hall Hotel, a former grand manor house built in 1830 as the family home of its current owner, Sir Hugh Blackett. The original grounds were laid out by 'Capability' Brown, the famous landscape architect. Jonathan Gaunt, designer of Linden Hall, reconfigured a number of greens and holes, most notably on the wonderful 18th. He is clearly a very capable designer.

The fairways are lush, the greens true, water (including the fast flowing River Pont) is used extensively to create interesting and testing hazards, and the presentation of the course is superb. The whole course is dotted with lovely old trees (some older than 100 years) augmented by large areas of new plantings.

There is a wonderful sense of space at Matfen thanks to the wide fairways and long views across the grounds. The whole course is immaculate and there is a number of really testing holes. We loved the creative use made of the water and the ha-ha as hazards, the old trees, the riggs and furrows across some of the fairways, and the birdlife. There is a real feeling of playing on the grounds of a grand manor. A truly lovely golf course.

Playability

The wide open fairways tempt you to believe you have a real chance of a good score. However, if our experience is any guide, the course seems to always frustrate your ambition by its length, wide expanses of rough grass and water challenges.

The sense of optimism that you start with is encouraged by the benign 1st (but be alert for the ha-ha just short of the green) and your first impression of the 2nd. On the latter you start pleasantly enough along a wide downhill fairway, but then you are called on to make an approach shot to a small green over the ha-ha. This is protected by large trees on both sides and there is a drop to the rear. The 5th is a long par 3 with a well-protected green set uphill. The 6th is a long par 5. The drive is from an elevated tee to a fairway that doglegs to the left. Trees block the direct line to the green and, for the approach shot, there is a nest of bunkers on the left side of the fairway and water some distance to the right. The green has flanking bunkers.

The 7th is one of Matfen's best. Your drive skirts a lake to the right, and a straight shot could find one of the three fairway bunkers 180 yards out on the right. To the left is a stand of tall trees about 160 yards from the tee. But as with the 2nd, the problems really start when you approach the green. This is elevated, has a deep gully in front, and is surrounded by bunkers. On the 9th, a lake runs to the right for 150 yards of the hole's length – a wayward shot from the tee could find it easily. But there is no safety to the left where there is a 60-yard-long bunker 190 yards out and a stand of trees a little ahead. There is a stream behind the well-bunkered green.

The 10th is a short par 3, but there is a stream in front of the tee, and along the left side of the fairway. The green slopes to the water and has three bunkers. At the 12th, the fairway is uphill and doglegs left. Within reach of a very good drive are a fairway bunker on the right and, to the left, a nest of six fairway bunkers and a stand of large trees. The undulating green is tucked to the right and has two bunkers on each side. The 14th is SI 1 and a long par 4. The drive is over a stream 140 yards out and there are two fairway bunkers on the left 230 yards on. A band of trees runs along the right side. The second shot requires a decision: go for the green and risk the stream about 20 yards in front, or lay up. The 15th offers multiple hazards: fairway bunkers to left and right about 200 yards out; a stream directly in front of the green. The green has three bunkers and a large tree to the front.

The 16th is one of the course's great holes – and for us the hardest, though SI 7. You need a good drive to carry over water and to have a clear shot to the green because of trees on the left corner about 170 yards out. Watch for the fairway bunker on the right about 240 yards from the tee. The approach shot is uphill and towards a simply horrid nest of seven bunkers in direct line to the narrow green. This is a picturesque hole: the hotel is ahead and the vista is grand. But the bunkering is awesome. The 17th is a long par 3 requiring a shot over a stream running diagonally in front and to the left of the green. Two fairway bunkers and a stand of mature trees are in play to the right of the green. At the 18th you are now heading back to the hotel but with a task still to do. You need a strong shot to the fairway (over water) to have a clear shot to the green. As you walk by the stream and pond you have just cleared (or not, as the case may be), enjoy the swans and geese nesting on the island. Mature trees and a large bunker block the right side to a green tucked to the left.

Hospitality

Matfen does a good job of making visitors welcome but they are asked to book their tee times in advance of arrival. There are restrictions on play at weekends between 8.00am and 10am. The Keeper's Lodge, a new

clubhouse building behind the 1st hole, has a well equipped pro-shop, extremely comfortable change/ locker rooms (with showers) and bar and meal facilities. A Half Way Hatch from the bar to a patio with table and seats offers players the chance to buy a snack and drink before teeing off on the 10th. A nine-hole par 3 course and a driving range provide welcome practice opportunities. Buggies are available for hire.

MORPETH

Contact

Phone: (01670) 504942
Fax: (01670) 504918
Mail: Morpeth Golf Club, The Common, Morpeth, NE 61 2BT

The Course

18 holes, 5834 yards, par 71, as played from the yellow tees.

Hole	Par	Length	Hole	Par	Length
1	4	241	10	5	548
2	4	420	11	4	365
3	5	466	12	4	332
4	3	170	13	4	293
5	4	440	14	3	163
6	5	465	15	4	294
7	4	344	16	4	268
8	3	137	17	3	132
9	4	381	18	4	375

Aesthetics

Morpeth is a mature parkland course designed by Harry Vardon. It was first established in 1906 and expanded to 18 holes in 1923.

It is a pretty and well-presented parkland course with both new and established trees, large true greens, lush turf fairways, and some particularly engaging holes. There are plenty of well-placed bunkers, some of which

are deep sided. Many first, and some second, shots are blind (be alert to the need to ring the bells at greens that signal the all clear for following players). Much of the course is crossed by riggs and furrows that prevent ball roll and give an uneven lie.

Morpeth is a pleasure to play. It's beautifully maintained, and offers all the benefits expected from a mature parkland course.

Playability

Morpeth has a good mix of hard and easier holes that give you a fair chance of a good score if you play well. The course is reasonably easy to walk except for two steep uphill holes (11th and 13th).

The following are the holes we enjoyed most. At the 3rd, a reasonably short par 5, you meet plenty of challenge. For the first half of the hole the fairway slopes steeply to the left towards two ditches. A deep gully bisects the fairway and OOB runs along the full length to the right. The green slopes from back to front and is protected by bunkers on two sides. The 5th is real beauty – SI 2 and the longest par 4. The green is blind for the drive; there is a well-placed fairway bunker to the left about 210 yards out from the tee and a large tree to the right of the fairway blocking a direct shot to the green. There is a steep slope to the left and rear of the green, and a road (OOB) close by on the other side for the last 100 yards or so.

The road (OOB) runs to the right of the fairway at the 6th. Here, the first shot is blind up a rise to a post. Having reached the top of the rise the fairway runs downhill. There is a fairway bunker to the right 128 yards in front of the green. The green is protected by three bunkers and there are trees to the rear. Ahead of the drive at the 7th waits a nest of three fairway bunkers on the left side and one to the right. The green is protected by four bunkers: one 40 yards out on the right, two on the green's right and one to its left. There are also shrubs behind. At the 9th, the fairway is tight for the drive because of trees to the left and a ditch to the right. The second shot is reasonably clear but watch for the hidden fairway bunker on the left about 40 yards out from the hard-to-read green.

The 10th is the longest par 5. The fairway doglegs slightly to the right making the drive blind. A reachable fairway bunker sits on the left side and trees intrude on the other side. OOB runs along the right side to the green. Another fairway bunker lies ahead of the green on the left side. The 11th is another fine hole. The first shot is blind to a post uphill to a fairway that slopes to the left and has deep riggs that stop ball roll. From the top of the hill, your shot is downhill over fairway bunkers on the right and left. Anything to the right will almost certainly find trees. The green is flanked by bunkers, is two-tiered and hard to read. The view of the Simonside Hills from the top offers some consolation for any shortfall in stroke making. Take note of the seat donated by ex-members with the gloating message: "Sit here and think of us in Spain. Lots of sun. No more rain."

At the 13th your drive is over a ditch up a steep hill to a plateau green. The second shot is typically from an uphill lie and must miss deep fairway bunkers about 15 yards out from the front of the green. The green slopes sharply from back to front. It's only a short par 4, but a struggle nonetheless. The 14th requires a shot from an elevated tee to a green obscured by trees on the left with three bunkers guarding the approach to the right. There is a stand of trees to the rear of the green, so don't overshoot. The 16th is a short par 4, but the fairway is constricted by trees pressing in to the right and OOB (a road) to the left. There are also two reachable bunkers on the left. The green is set down and is guarded by three bunkers, and trees and ditch on the left. The shot to the green at the 17th is over a deep gully (with ditch) and a high-sided bunker. The green has flanking bunkers (the one on the right is deep), OOB close to the rear, and is partly hidden by a stand of trees.

Hospitality

The staff and members are welcoming and friendly, and the club's full facilities are available to visitors. However, Morpeth is a popular course with a strong membership so it can be very busy, so always check in advance to arrange a tee time. Also, access to non-members is restricted on weekends and bank holidays. There are no buggies for hire.

PONTELAND

Contact

Phone: (01661) 822689
Fax: (01661) 860077
e-mail: secretary@thepontelandgolfclub.co.uk
Mail: Ponteland Golf Club, 53 Bell Villas, NE20 9BD

The Course

18 holes, 6287 yards, par 72, played from yellow tees.

Hole	Par	Length	Hole	Par	Length
1	4	418	10	4	330
2	3	167	11	4	398
3	4	339	12	4	316
4	4	322	13	5	482
5	4	334	14	4	364
6	4	402	15	3	137
7	3	161	16	4	443
8	5	470	17	4	291
9	4	443	18	5	470

Aesthetics

Ponteland is another lovely mature parkland course. It was opened in 1927 initially as a nine-hole course with a second nine added in 1931. The original design work was done by the then professional at Gosforth Golf Club, Harry Fernie, but it has been continually reworked ever since. One aspect of this has been the planting of thousands of trees, including oak, beech, chestnut, birch, pine and poplar. Since 1967 the tree planting programme has been under the supervision of the Forestry Commission.

The course we see today is the product of the past 75 years of constant enhancement. While delightfully framed by mature and maturing trees, the fairways have not been confined into narrow avenues as is often the case with parkland courses. This gives a feeling of space – of being in an open park – but without any sense of intrusion by other players. The fairways are in superb conditions, as are the large greens. The bunkers are well placed and often difficult to escape, and the drainage seems to be excellent.

The course is only four miles from Newcastle, and a mile from Newcastle Airport. However, you wouldn't know it. Apart from a distant glimpse of the airport, and the passage overhead of the occasional plane, there is nothing urban in view. Your views are principally of surrounding farmland. There are deep riggs and furrows around the course despite some work to remove them by cross-ploughing. These blunt ball run, and on some holes funnel the ball towards danger.

Playability

Ponteland is one of the longest courses in Northumberland, with long par 4s (four over 400 yards), plenty of cleverly placed bunkers and deep riggs and furrows. Nevertheless, it's a fair course, with fairways of generous

width, giving players of all standards hope for a good card. The course is largely level and easy to negotiate.

The 2nd, the longest par 3, requires a shot over a ditch about 140 yards from the tee to a two-tier green sloping back to front. The green is heavily bunkered – two on each side and a large one in front. At the 4th, the first shot is blind uphill to a fairway that slopes towards trees and OOB. The lateral riggs may run the ball in the wrong direction. The green slopes back to front and is protected by three bunkers, one 20 yards in front to the right. The 6th is a long par 4, and SI 2. The drive is slightly downhill to a fairway sloping to the right and OOB. About 240 yards out from the tee the fairway is constricted by trees on both sides. The sloping green has the usual complement of deep bunkers.

The fairway on the 8th, par 5, is cleverly defended by bunkers. There is one on either side within the 180 to 220 yard range, two in the centre of the fairway 100 yards ahead of these, and another on the centre right 30 yards further ahead. The green slopes gently from back to front and has flanking bunkers. The 9th, the longest par 4, requires a blind uphill drive to a fairway corrugated by riggs. Fairway bunkers await on the left (160 yards) and right (200 yards). The second shot is also blind, but downhill. The green has two bunkers on the right and another on the left.

The 10th is a reasonably long par 4, but the fairway doglegs sharply to the right about 230 yards out from the tee. The corner is constricted by trees on two sides and a fairway bunker on the right – anything short and right is blocked by trees. The sloping green is well protected by bunkers. The 11th is a strong par 4 with the drive uphill into deep riggs. Fairway bunkers sit about 20 yards out from the green on two sides in reach of the second shot. The 13th is the longest par 5. The drive is blind uphill to a pole at which point the fairway sweeps to the left. In reach, for the approach shots, are a band of mature trees to the left and a fairway bunker on the right. The sloping green has bunkers on both sides.

The 14th is SI 5. Deep lateral riggs and well-placed fairway bunkers at 190 and 240 yards present difficulties here. About 200 yards from the tee the fairway turns left and runs downhill – trees block the path to the green for a shot to the left. The large green slopes to the front and has flanking bunkers. The 15th is a short par 3, but with OOB close on the right of the fairway and green. There are four large bunkers around the green, including a large one directly in front.

The 16th is the second longest par 4 and SI 1. A direct line to the fairway is over an intruding corner of hedgerow and trees. To the left is a hidden fairway bunker 200 yards from the tee. The green is surrounded by bunkers. While the 17th is a short par 4, it seems to play much longer. The left side of the fairway is blocked by three bunkers in the range of 140 to 190 yards, and by an intrusion of trees, 230 yards on the right. The green has two deep bunkers on the right side and two smaller bunkers on the left. Distance is not an issue at the 18th, a short par 5. However, there is a fairway bunker on the left (210 yards) and another in the centre (175 yards). At about 300 yards from the tee the fairway doglegs to the right around a stand of trees blocking a direct shot to the green. Another fairway bunker sits in the middle about 50 yards from the green which is further protected by bunkers on either side. The green is under the clubhouse bar windows so there is pressure for a grandstand finish.

Hospitality

Ponteland has a large membership and can be very busy so it's imperative that you contact the course to arrange a tee time. Visitors are welcome from Tuesday to Thursday. The staff are welcoming, rightly proud of their fine course and very helpful (my interest in seeing a history of the course led staff to conduct a search that finally produced a copy which I was invited to keep). The facilities, especially for dining, are excellent, as is the pro-shop. You will need to ask to gain access to the locker rooms.

PRUDHOE

Contact

Phone: (01661) 836188 for bookings
e-mail: prudhoegolfclub.co.uk
Mail: Eastwood Park, Prudhoe, Northumberland, NE42 5DX

The Course

18 holes, 5618 yards, par 69, as played from the yellow tees.

Hole	Par	Length	Hole	Par	Length
1	4	333	10	4	440
2	4	297	11	3	163
3	4	374	12	4	274
4	4	324	13	3	161
5	4	260	14	5	542
6	4	322	15	3	130
7	3	165	16	4	324
8	4	347	17	4	348
9	4	405	18	4	409

Aesthetics

Prudhoe is a mature (1930) parkland course set in the Tyne Valley about 12 miles west of Newcastle and in the midst of its commuter belt. However, once on the course there is no urban intrusion whatsoever. Instead there is the silence of the country; a panorama of mature and young trees (birch, ash, beech and conifers); wide, well-grassed fairways and fine long view of the Tyne hills. The course is hilly but, with a few exceptions, the climbs are gentle. It's simply an exceptionally attractive course – it's particularly beautiful in Autumn with its trees full of colour.

The only problem we could see with Prudhoe is that it may well be wet underfoot after heavy rain. However, this is to be expected with most of the parkland courses.

Playability

At first glance Prudhoe looks reasonably easy. It's only 5618 yards long and the wide fairways, with their small internal trees, are generally forgiving of errant shots; the rough is relatively manicured. The bunkers are shallow and there is no water in play. However, it's a par 69, has some really hard holes (and none you would call really easy), three of the par 4s are over 400 yards, the greens have enough slope to really test your putting skills, and many first shots are blind.

The 2nd, a short par 4, demands an accurate drive. It is blind, steeply uphill and through a narrow 'tunnel' formed by large trees on two sides. Close to the right the large trees are OOB. Once you are on the fairway you will find it turns right and continues downhill to a large green with flanking bunkers – another bunker sits to the front of the green to the right. At the 3rd the first shot is blind uphill to a pole – the second would be blind also unless the drive is very long. The green is tucked to the right behind a stand of trees. There is another stand of trees on the other side of the corner and a fairway bunker. Visible here are riggs and furrows that continue for the next few holes. The 6th is SI 14. The drive (across the 3rd fairway) is blind downhill. The fairway doglegs left to a sloping green flanked by bunkers.

While the 7th, par 3, is only 165 yards it plays longer as the first shot is uphill to a guide pole. The large green slopes to the rear and has a bunker on the right side. At the 8th, the drive is blind uphill to a pole to a fairway that has a slope to the left towards a line of trees. From the pole the second shot is downhill to a sloping green flanked by bunkers and with large trees close by to the rear.

The 10th is the longest par 4. The fairway runs downhill and turns to the right. About 100 yards out from the green a long bunker runs across the fairway to catch the second shot. The large green has trees close by to the rear and the usual flanking bunkers. The 12th is a short par 4, but the blind uphill drive is to a plateau green tucked to the right behind a stand of trees with a ditch in front. The 13th, par 3, is steeply uphill with bunkers in front (deep) and on both sides. The green slopes to the front right.

The par 5, 14th is an exceptional hole – Prudhoe's best. It is long at 542 yards and there is real trouble ahead for the second and third shots. Both are blind, because the green is set uphill sharply to the right behind a hill. There are two options for the second shot: continue along the fairway towards two bunkers sitting at the bottom of the right hand hillside, or take a risk and cut the corner over the hill. If the last option is taken there are two bunkers in direct line to the green and trees to the right. Whatever the option the plateau green – with its slope back down the hill – is hard to hold.

15th Hole, par 3

The 16th – a short par 4 – requires a well placed drive to allow a clear shot to a green tucked around a corner to the right. The corner is protected by a stand of mature trees and two fairway bunkers on the left. The green is slightly elevated with bunkers on both sides. Approaching the green you must be alert to players driving off the 17th tee over the 16th fairway.

The 17th tee is set high to the side of the 16th green with a wonderful outlook to the north. The green is obscured on the left behind trees, so to ensure a clear shot go to the high-sided right hand of the fairway. The green is flat

Prudhoe, 17th tee

with a bunker on the right. The 18th is a long par 4. The drive is uphill to a pole with OOB and two fairway bunkers on the left. At the top of the hill it's straight ahead to a green that slopes to the front.

Hospitality

The only problems we can see for the visitor is that the course is very busy, no doubt a consequence of how pleasant it is to play and its location close to Newcastle and its dormitory suburbs. Visitors are welcome except on competition days. The pro-shop, while small, is very well stocked with all necessary golf equipment and the clubhouse is comfortable with all the facilities, including meals and bar snacks.

STOCKSFIELD

Contact

Phone: (01661) 843041
Fax: (01661) 843046
e-mail: info@sgcgolf.co.uk
Mail: New Ridley Road, Stocksfield, Northumberland, NE43 7RE

The Course

18 holes, 5594 yards, par 68, played from yellow tees.

Hole	Par	Length	Hole	Par	Length
1	4	337	10	3	168
2	4	306	11	4	332
3	3	173	12	4	320
4	4	297	13	4	380
5	4	335	14	3	165
6	4	313	15	4	350
7	4	363	16	4	349
8	4	390	17	4	420
9	4	462	18	3	134

Aesthetics

This is one of the most interesting parkland courses in Northumberland. Set in the lovely Tyne Valley, it is really two courses in one. The original nine holes were laid out in 1913 with a further nine added in 1980 to a Frank Pennick design, and they couldn't be more different.

You play the newer nine holes first. These run up, down and along the side of a heavily wooded and hilly land. Minimal clearance of the old woodland when laying out the course means the fairways are set in avenues of beautiful old oak, ash, birch and beech trees. The large trees are a constant danger and the fairways tight, indeed the sound of balls pinging off trees is an acoustic background to these holes. There are water hazards on most holes, and the fairways slope steeply. As would be expected from a designer who specialized in adding difficulty, the green positions are placed in order to challenge.

The older, original, nine holes also run on hilly land. The fairways are wide and well manicured and most trees, while pretty, are quite small (because of the clay base). The views from these holes are lovely – east and west along the Tyne Valley and north to the Cheviots and Border country. The sense of openness gives the confidence to really blast away.

We strongly recommend Stocksfield. It's a picturesque, hilly course with glorious large trees on the first nine, an abundance of lateral water hazards, slippery fairways, and clever green positions. The fine views are a bonus. Its only fault is that the first nine tend to be boggy after rain due to leakage from the hillside and its natural poor drainage (despite the club's best efforts).

Playability

As suggested above, the two nines of the course play quite differently. In the first nine there is a greater need for accuracy because of the trees and green positions, and there is more opportunity to damage your card. The second nine is more forgiving because of its wider and more open fairways. The back nine gives you some chance to compensate for any trouble on the first. While the course is relatively short, with no par 5s, many of the holes are uphill thereby making them play longer.

Stocksfield may be a little physically taxing for some, but it's a beautiful and interesting course, especially the first nine, and therefore worth the effort or the hire of a buggy.

The course has some truly great holes. The 1st is one. The first shot, though blind, isn't an issue; the second is. The green is small and set against a fence and OOB. In front is a deep and wide gully, with a lateral water hazard at the base. There is a bunker to the rear and a reasonably safe area to the right, but all of this is academic unless you clear the gully. Being downhill the 2nd, a short par 4, shouldn't be a problem. But the fairway slopes to the right and the sloping green is tucked close to the trees on the left side. The 3rd, a reasonably long par 3, requires a shot over a gully and lateral water hazard to a two-tier green with OOB close to the rear.

You would expect the 4th, a short par 4, to be a breeze, but somehow it isn't. The first shot is from a tree-lined tee to a sloping fairway with a reachable lateral water hazard 220 yards out. The fairway doglegs to the right and the two-tier green is well bunkered. At the 5th, another short par 4, the first shot is out through a gap between large trees to a sharply sloping fairway. The second shot is downhill and over a pond. The two-tier green has a large bunker on the left. Your tee shot is blind at the 7th, but the real problem is with the approach shot. The small green is set over a deep gully and set back close to OOB with trees on both sides. This is an awesome shot for all but those with great control.

The 8th, SI 2, is a long par 4. The drive is from a tree-lined tee to a post. A fence and trees (OOB) run along the left side of the fairway and you have to stay close to these to avoid the slope to the right. From the post the fairway opens out and runs downhill. The green is tucked into the left corner close to the trees. There is a lateral water hazard running diagonally across the fairway about 70 yards out from the green.

You start the back nine with a par 3 requiring a shot downhill over a water hazard running across the front of the green. At the 11th, the drive is blind uphill to a gap between large trees on each side of the fairway – there is a gully in reach. From the post the fairway doglegs to the left. The green is uphill and tucked to the left. The 13th is a hard hole because it's a long par 4 and uphill (hence SI1). The green is set back against a fence and trees (OOB) and has bunkers on two sides. The 14th is a short par 3, but the hole is steeply uphill. A fence and trees run to the right (OOB). The elevated green has bunkers on two sides. The green (and the next tee) are at a high point of the course and accordingly have wonderful views in all directions.

At the 15th the tee shot is downhill from an elevated tee to a fairway sloping to the left. A fence (OOB) is close to the right. At the bottom of the hill large trees block the approach to the green on two sides. At the 16th you hit uphill to a post to a sloping fairway that doglegs to the right. There are two reachable fairway bunkers on the right and the elevated and sloping green is flanked by the bunkers. The 17th is a long par 4. The tee shot is downhill along an open fairway that doglegs to the left: a large tree marks the corner. The green slopes from back to right and has a steep slope in front.

Hospitality

As is usual in Northumberland you will receive a warm reception here; the staff have obvious pride in the quality of their course and make visitors very welcome. However, you can't play on Wednesdays or during certain hours at the weekend. The very pleasant clubhouse has full locker room, bar and meal facilities and a snooker table. There is also a well-equipped pro-shop. Entrance to the clubhouse is by key pad, thus blocking free visitor access, but this is not intended to be inhospitable, and the pro-shop staff will let you in on request.

MOORLAND COURSES

Our final category of courses takes us into the higher, exposed ground of Northumberland. These courses share some features with the links: they have a sense of space, and have been designed around nature, not over it. They are usually devoid of trees other than those haphazardly and infrequently arranged by nature. While their fairways may be well turfed, well mown and neat they lack the manicured state of the parkland course, and they make extensive use of nature's own hazards in combination with those introduced by the designer. The fairways are defined not by trees, but by low vegetation such as gorse, heather, and other native vegetation. They can be boggy after rain. All the courses featured here have fine long views of the surrounding countryside, and give the impression of being on top of the county looking down.

The two clearest moorland courses are Wooler (9 hole) and Haltwhistle. However, it's a matter of contention whether Bellingham and Allendale, both self-described as parkland courses, are not in fact moorland courses. Others courses such as Alnwick and Bamburgh have moorland characteristics.

ALLENDALE

Contact

Phone: (0191) 2648383
e-mail: info@warmseal.co.uk
Mail: Allendale Golf Club, High Studdon, Allenheads Rd, NE47 9DH

The Course

Nine holes with alternate tees for 18 holes. Playing all 18 holes the distance is 4501 yards, par 66, played from the yellow tees.

The first nine is the longer at 2318 yards with the back nine being 2183 yards. Both are par 33. Seven of the holes are played from different tee boxes, altering both length and angle, and in two cases par.

This is a relatively new course established in 1992. However, the club has a much longer history having played at other courses since about 1906, the last at Thornley Gate from 1923.

Hole	Par	Length	Hole	Par	Length
1	4	410	10	4	336
2	3	118	11	3	86
3	3	187	12	3	132
4	4	340	13	4	366
5	4	251	14	4	251
6	4	312	15	4	392
7	4	251	16	4	251
8	4	300	17	3	147
9	3	149	18	4	222

Aesthetics

We take issue with Allendale's self-description as a "hilly parkland course" and instead have designated it a moorland course, a description with which the members with whom we discussed this agreed. It's set high on moorland some 1000 feet above sea level on the southern side of the Tyne Valley overlooking the Dale of Allen with the Cheviots dominating the northern skyline. The view is simply magnificent in all directions. Indeed, on a clear day you can see the Cumbrian Mountains.

The fairways are open and lushly turfed, there are some bands of lovely mature and young trees in places, and a couple of deep gullies add to the character and difficulty of the course. The greens are small and slippery, but thankfully there are only three bunkers on the whole course.

Playability

This is a very challenging and physical course with a couple of memorable holes – the 17th 'Grand Canyon' being the best. The course runs along, down and up the side of a steep hill and is devoid of level ground. What passes for relatively level ground has a marked sideways slope. Many first, and some second, shots are blind and in dry conditions holding the fairway slope could prove difficult. The only real downside is that the course is boggy after rain and we recommend that you leave it for when conditions are dry.

It's a short course but this is offset by the terrain and the course's low par. Par 4s dominate, but only one exceeds 400 yards; the shortest is 222 yards. The par 3s range from 86 yards to 187 yards.

A few holes stand out. The 3rd is a prime example of the type of challenge the course presents. It's a long par 3 almost straight down a steep hill with trees and a gully on the right and a stone wall (OOB) and band of rough to the left. A small gully runs across the fairway about 40 yards in front of the green. The green has a steep slope on three sides. Played as the 12th, the distance is less but there is a band of trees obscuring the left side of the green.

The fairway at the 4th, a par 4, slopes sharply from right to left towards a band of rough. A stand of mature trees runs to the right side and there is a row of hawthorn bushes and a ditch running up the middle. The green also slopes from right to left. The tee for the 13th is set uphill and the hole runs along a parallel fairway. For most of its distance it, too, slopes from right to left. It has a gully to negotiate and, towards the green, flanking trees that must be negotiated to reach the green safely.

The drive at the 6th, a par 4, to a green marked by a pole is uphill to a fairway that slopes from left to right. A deep gully with its band of mature trees is within reach of a short drive, but can be cleared with a good one. Thereafter it's a short shot to the green but this could be blind depending on the length of the drive. Played from the 15th (SI 1) the hole is 80 yards longer which makes finding the gully more likely.

The 8th is a short par 4. The drive is to the corner of a deep, tree-lined gully where the fairway doglegs to the left. To have a clear shot to the green you must be to the right of the fairway but this brings the rough into play.

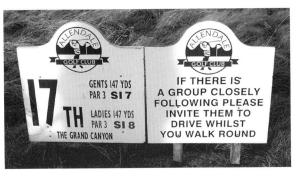

Playing this hole as the 17th tee presents a different view of the hole. This is 'Grand Canyon', Allendale's signature hole. It's much shorter (only 147

yards) and thus par 3, but it's an extraordinary hole. In front of the tee is a deep gorge with a large planting of tall conifers on the far bank which must be cleared to reach the barely visible green behind. In reality this is not a difficult hole as the landing area is open and large, but the trees present the kind of brain-numbing obstacle that causes 'duffed' shots and wrong club selection because you can't put it out of your mind and simply 'go the distance'.

Hospitality

Visitors are welcome, including at weekends, and the clubhouse is new; built in 1996 with a donation from the Lottery Sports Fund, it has a bar and changing facilities. However, when the clubhouse is unattended, which can happen with small clubs, there is no access to the interior other than to the vestibule where the honesty box is located.

We believe that if a course welcomes visitors when not attended, it should give them access to the basic amenities of a lavatory and a changing room. This is a curious omission in the case of a new clubhouse.

BELLINGHAM

Contact

Phone: Secretary (01434) 220530
Clubhouse (01434) 220152
e-mail: admin@bellinghamgolfclub.com
Mail: Bellingham Golf Club, Boggle Hole, Bellingham, NE48 2DT

The Course

18 holes, 5902 yards, par 70, as played from the yellow tees.

Hole	Par	Length	Hole	Par	Length
1	4	362	10	4	376
2	4	267	11	5	523
3	4	331	12	4	344
4	3	116	13	4	354
5	4	324	14	3	130
6	4	355	15	4	401
7	4	396	16	4	382
8	5	546	17	3	155
9	3	170	18	4	370

Aesthetics

Bellingham was founded in 1893 as a nine-hole course on land owned by the Duke of Northumberland. In 1996 the Club purchased adjoining Boggle Hole Farm to build a second nine holes using development funding from the European Community and English Lottery. The two parts of the course are indistinguishable. Don't worry that 'boggle' means 'ghost':

we didn't see any evidence that the course is haunted, although strangely enough we did lose a few balls mysteriously! Bellingham is described in the AA golf course guide as a "rolling parkland course". We say "rubbish" to this; it is undeniably a *moorland* course, set high on moorland overlooking the Tyne Valley with wonderful long views across the countryside. The location engenders a pleasing sense of rural isolation and peace.

The course is steep in parts and hilly in others, and many of the fairways have plenty of sideways slope. This terrain gives the course character. The fairways are lushly turfed and mostly very open, the trees along the fairways are still small, the grass rough is generous and could be a real problem if allowed any length, and the greens are reasonably level and true. There is good bunkering throughout but this is not too punitive. A distinguishing, and pretty, feature is a stream, for most of its length set in a deep gully edged with large trees, which meanders through and alongside the course. While it's in play on some holes, it's more a visual attraction than a hazard.

Playability

Bellingham is a very fair course thanks to its generous fairways and level greens, but it's not easy. Indeed, some holes are quite intimidating, posing a lot of trouble for any inaccuracy. Wind could be a problem and the course is somewhat physical (thankfully, buggies are available for hire if required).

It has a good mix of holes with two quite long par 5s, twelve par 4s (only one over 400 yards), and four par 3s (mostly tricky).

We found the back nine the most challenging, and interesting, but the first had some favourites also. The 2nd, a par 4, is a good example. The drive is from an elevated tee with the road (OOB) on the right and the stream about 190 yards out. The safe approach is to play to the left over a small hill and thereafter to chip up to the slightly elevated green. The 4th, a short par 3, could wreck your card early on as it runs steeply downhill over the stream to a green set down behind a huge bunker with a gully (OOB) close by to the rear and right. The 5th, a short par 4, is uphill. There is a gully to the right and two fairway bunkers on the left. The elevated green is set to the left around a corner.

The 7th, a strong par 4 (and SI 2), is also blind uphill towards a hidden green marked by a pole. There are two fairway bunkers to the left and the green is protected by three bunkers.

You should count on being ahead of the card as you start the back nine as there is some serious business ahead. The 11th, par 5, is blind uphill and requires two good shots to see the green, set low and marked by a pole. A line of trees to the left is OOB and there are three fairway bunkers to the right. The tee for the 12th is the highest point of the course. The first couple of shots are downhill and there is a dry gully with trees and rough to the right in reach of a wayward drive. The fairway narrows as you approach the green, which is set down at the bottom of a steep hill with a stream running across the front and to the right and a bunker at the back. There are large trees to the left. The 14th is an awesome par 3. It's only short, but the shot is steeply downhill to a green that allows little margin for error; it is over deep, short, rolling gullies with large areas of rough and a deep bunker to the front left. OOB is over the fence at the rear and two further bunkers to the right and rear. It's an absolute joy if you hit the right shot.

The 15th is a long par 4 and understandably SI 1. The drive is steeply uphill to a pole marking a fairly narrow landing area. On top of the hill, the second shot, also blind, must negotiate large trees to reach a steeply downhill green. Treat par as a birdie. The 17th, par 3, is across a deep gully to a green protected on three sides by bunkers.

The final hole is a cracker. The drive is blind across the same gully to a narrow, steeply sloping fairway with a band of trees to the left. A band of rough runs along the topside of the fairway from where the green is unsighted. Consequently, the best approach is along the bottom of the fairway. All this is in sight of the members in the clubhouse, and trouble still to come. The green is tucked to the right, and if approached from the bottom of the fairway, is steeply uphill. Two deep gullies lie in front. This is a truly superb finishing hole.

Hospitality

Bellingham is a very welcoming club and visitors may play all week. The clubhouse is warm and comfortable with all the amenities visitors would expect, including bar and catering facilities. In addition to these there are fine views from the lounge and the opportunity to enjoy the discomfort of players finishing the 18th. There is a driving range at the course and, as mentioned earlier, buggies are available for hire.

HALTWHISTLE

Contact

Phone: (01697) 747367 or (01434) 344000
Fax: (01434) 344311
Mail: Haltwhistle Golf Club, Wallend Farm, CA6 7HN

The Course

18 holes, 5250 yards, par 69, as played from the yellow tees.

Aesthetics

Hole	Par	Length	Hole	Par	Length
1	3	184	10	4	306
2	4	320	11	4	282
3	4	282	12	3	155
4	4	250	13	3	160
5	4	380	14	5	505
6	3	160	15	4	355
7	4	358	16	4	369
8	5	420	17	4	288
9	4	325	18	3	149

It has to be said that Haltwhistle was a complete surprise to us. It's a little away from the more heavily populated areas of the county and, perhaps for this reason, it hasn't had the exposure to golfing circles it deserves. Of all the golfers with whom we associate only one had played it, and it was on his recommendation that we made the trip. His description, which was highly complimentary, didn't do it justice; it was much better. We urge all golfing visitors to make the journey, which in any event takes you into the heart of 'Hadrian's Wall country'.

Haltwhistle is a moorland course built by its members in 1967, on high land atop the northern ridge of the Tyne Valley. In short, it's a truly memorable golf course.

Why? The first reason is the challenge that it offers, but more on this later. The second is the wonderful scenery visible from all points. To the north there are long views to the Northumberland National Park and Spadeadam Forest; and to the south, the Pennines. In between are striking views of the surrounding countryside. Finally, Haltwhistle is the only golf course of which we are aware that sits on the path of Hadrian's Wall. The Wall's course and remains can be seen clearly coming down from the Great Whin Sill to the north into the village of Greenhead. They are lost there but reappear on the northern edge of the course and cross along its western boundary to be part of its hazard. This is a wonderful historical adornment to the course.

Playability

Haltwhistle is a hilly course and most holes are either steeply uphill or downhill, thus making it physically tiring. The fairways and greens are very good – the last being large and often with tricky slopes. There are a very few (shallow) bunkers, but there are gullies and ditches traversing the fairways, and the fairways' steep slopes, lateral and vertical, demand careful course management and positive play. Drainage appears to be very good, probably because of many years of drains improvement.

It's hard to pick out the holes deserving honourable mention as most are particularly engaging. The 1st is the longest par 3. The drive is from an elevated tee over a gully and would be particularly difficult if played into the prevailing westerly wind. The remains of the Wall run the entire left length of the fairway. The green slopes to the front and there is a bunker on the left front. From the tee at the 2nd, you have a clear view of the Wall's course running down from the Whin Sill, and the ruin of an old pele tower (Thirlwall Castle) overlooking Greenhead village. The drive is downhill over the Wall's course towards two lateral drainage ditches and three large trees about 200 yards out. There is a double green (shared with the 17th hole).

The 4th is the shortest par 4 but is nevertheless SI 2. The drive is downhill through a gap in a field wall about 100 yards out, and the gap is blocked by a tree in the centre. These negotiated, the dogleg fairway runs uphill to an elevated green. The 5th, a 380 yard par 4, is SI 1. From an elevated tee at the highest point of the course the fairway doglegs right (OOB on this side to the green) – the drive is downhill blind to a pole. The approach shot is to a green with extreme slope back to front and has a band of trees close by on the right. The 6th, par 3, is a modest 160 yards. There is a ditch on the right side that turns in front of the two-tier green. The 8th is the shorter of Haltwhistle's two par 5s. The drive is downhill through trees and, if a reasonable shot, will land in an area that slopes to OOB on the left. Thereafter it's steeply uphill to a green that slopes downhill. The last 150 yards are a hard slog.

The 11th is another short par 4 but the drive is downhill to a tree in the middle of the fairway and a drain at its lowest point. Here the fairway turns left where a planting of trees can obscure the green. The 12th, a par 3, is a fun hole. Only 155 yards but the green is set well downhill with large trees and OOB to the rear. The 13th is another short par 3 but the green is set on top of a steep hill, defended by a wall about 20 yards in front, and its slopes downhill.

The 14th is a good length par 5. At first the fairway runs steeply downhill to a flat area that slopes to the right, then a little uphill, before downhill for the last 120 or so yards. The green slopes right towards a bunker. The 17th is a short par 4 but is uphill to a narrow fairway running atop a ridge that initially slopes to the right towards a band of rough. The double green slopes to the left. The 18th, par 3, is only 149 yards but the shot is steeply downhill to a backward sloping green with trees and a bunker at the rear.

Hospitality

The modest but comfortable clubhouse is closed on Mondays, but even then it's unlocked to allow visitors to pay their green fees (there is an honesty box inside to receive the money) and to use the facilities. Visitors are made welcome by staff and members who are clearly proud to share their wonderful course, however they are asked not to play before 3pm on Sundays. Buggies are not available.

WOOLER

Contact

Phone: Secretary: (01668) 281631
　　　　Clubhouse (01668) 282135
Mail: Wooler Golf Club, Dodd Law, Doddington, NE71 6EA.

The Course

Nine holes, with alternative tees for 18 holes (6411 yards, par 72). Our distances and pars are from the white tees. The distances for each hole from the alternate tees vary, but the second nine is only 117 yards longer in total than the first. There are significant differences in length between the 7th (par 4) and 16th (par 3) holes.

Hole	Par	Length		Hole	Par	Length
1	4	326		10	4	363
2	4	315		11	4	342
3	3	134		12	3	141
4	5	565		13	5	587
5	4	371		14	4	349
6	4	304		15	4	332
7	4	316		16	3	201
8	4	432		17	5	492
9	4	429		18	4	412

Aesthetics

We have a particular affection for Wooler. It is the creation of the hard work of its members, who seem to do all the tasks, including the greenkeeping, themselves, and they have done a magnificent job. Further, we have been received with considerable kindness on the many times we have played there. But even if these factors were not an issue, we think it's simply a wonderful golf course.

Wooler winds its way up, down and across Dodd Law, a pinnacle on the edge of Glendale Valley. The views are magnificent: to the east the sea over the coastal plain, to the west the Cheviots (Cheviot, the highest point, is clearly visible), and to the north-west the Scottish borders. You feel you are on top of the world.

The fairways are a bit lean, but the greens are excellent. The ground is well drained for a moorland course and there is an abundance of gorse, bracken and grass rough.

Being only 9 holes is not an issue, as the 18 tees are located to ensure variety for a second round. Wind would be a problem or a challenge, depending on how you view your golf. The views are breathtaking and the greens are of a quality befitting a more expensive course.

In addition to its other virtues, Wooler lets you step back into the Iron Age. If you follow a track running out from the left side of the fairway on the 7th hole you will find Iron-Age rock carvings dating from around 2000 BC. A little on the right of this are the remains of an Iron-Age hillfort. There can be few golf holes in the world offering the attractions of this one.

Also, there is an abundance of wildlife including pheasants, hares, squirrels and deer. The quarry on the left of the 1st and 2nd holes provided much of the pink sandstone used in the grander old buildings of Edinburgh.

Playability

We have played Wooler in both still and windy conditions, and we might as well have been playing different courses! The course is never easy, but the wind plays havoc with loose shots and a far more defensive approach is required if balls are not to be lost, and strokes gained. The steep slopes of the fairways and the positioning of the greens would test the very best golfers. This is not a course, however, for the less mobile; it is very strenuous and tiring.

Wooler has more than any course's share of great holes. Ahead of the tee at the 2nd are two hawthorn trees and further on, where the fairway takes a sharp turn to the left, there is a stand of trees on the corner. The side of the hill (with bracken, rocks and deep grass) runs along the left of the fairway to the side of an elevated and sloping green. It's hard to get your ball to hold on the sloping green. This is SI 1 when played as the longer 10th hole from the alternate tee. The 3rd, par 3, has the tee on top of a hill with the shot downhill over rough to a green protected in the front by a drain. The 4th is the only par 5 on the 'front' nine. The drive is blind downhill to a fairway that doglegs to the right. The green is at the bottom of a steep and slippery hill.

The 5th is SI 2 (SI 9 from the slightly shorter 14th). The steepness of the uphill slope makes this a tough par 4. The green has two tiers and a band of trees at the rear and to the right. At the 6th the fairway doglegs to the left around a stand of trees about 180 yards out. These must be escaped to have a clear shot to the steeply elevated green. This sits against the side of a hill and has a grass bank to the left and a slope from back to front.

At the 7th, the tee is set high on the side of a hill with the first shot downhill to a wide fairway. Stay to the right as there is a hillock on the left that hides a green perched dangerously close to the edge of a cliff. But it's not only the golf that makes this hole memorable: from the tee there are magnificent 360 degree views of the Cheviots, Glendale Valley, surrounding countryside and the sea – the views from the green are even better. Seek out the Iron

Age rock carvings and hillfort to the left of the fairway. Here you have a great opportunity to ponder how marvellous it is to be playing golf in such a breathtaking setting.

The 8th is the longest par 4 from either tee. The first shot is downhill to a pole over an area of rough to the left. The green is visible for the second shot but the steepness of the slope, and the run into rough to its rear, make the approach shot difficult to judge. The 9th is another long par 4. You hit over about 100 yards of rough to a fairway sloping to OOB on the left. The fairway then doglegs sharply to the left to a green at the bottom of a steep hill. As with the previous hole, great care has to be taken with the approach shot as the green slopes to the back.

Hospitality

Visitors are welcome except on Tuesdays and Saturdays. The clubhouse is basic but comfortable and offers bar facilities. An honesty box operates if the clubhouse is shut.

Clubhouse
at
Wooler

SOME TIPS FOR VISITING GOLFERS

It's not our intention here to pretend that we are experts on the subject of a golfer's requirements while on a tour of Northumberland. However, having made some discoveries, and learnt a few lessons, we thought it appropriate to pass on the following tips to help smooth the visitor's path.

Yardages

The yardages given in the book are from the visitors' – usually *yellow* – tees except where stated otherwise. Unless told not to, or given express permission on request, visitors should expect to play off the visitors' tees.

Green Fees

We haven't given the green fees for each course because they change between summer and winter, weekdays and weekends, and annually. However, you can be assured that the fees are as low as you will find in Britain. At the time of writing most courses we feature charge less than £30 a round in summer (winter rates are lower).

Contacting the Courses

The courses we feature accept visitors willingly, but it's wise to contact them in advance to arrange a tee time. In summer there are generally restrictions on the times available on weekends and public holidays and on competition days during the week. But it's unusual not to find a time acceptable to you. In winter you will have no trouble booking a game, but it can be difficult to contact the club to confirm this as clubhouses may be unattended. This doesn't mean the course is closed, as usually an honesty box and some limited clubhouse access are available.

Discount Golf

There are two schemes operating that allow two to play for the price of one under certain conditions. These are '2-FORE-1' featured in the golf magazine '*Today's Golfer*', and the 'Green Fee Saver' sponsored by '*Bunkered*' magazine. Both magazines are sold widely in local newsagents. The first has more courses in Northumberland (and the rest of England) while the last focuses more on Scotland. At the time of writing the vouchers cost a few pounds plus a service fee. The savings they offer are considerable.

Vouchers can be ordered by mail or phone, and arrive promptly. The conditions attached are minimal and many prestigious courses are included. Since conditions, courses and voucher charges change from time to time they will not be detailed here, but visitors are strongly urged to avail themselves of the cost saving they allow.

Most of the courses described in the book accept the '2-FORE-1' vouchers and somewhat fewer the 'Green Fee Saver'. We have not attempted to identify which ones, because participation can change, so get the list from the companies to ensure currency. Each course attaches conditions to the days/times the vouchers can be used, so do check. Also, mention to the course when you book a tee time that you will be using a voucher to make sure that the conditions haven't changed. Don't be hesitant about using the vouchers as the subscribing clubs accept them without hesitation or discrimination.

On-Course Facilities

On-course lavatory facilities are rare and most courses don't bring you back to the clubhouse 'at the turn', so use the clubhouse facilities before you play. As there are no 'half-way' houses for refreshments, take water and snacks with you.

Motorised Carts or 'Buggies'

The visitor may experience a definitional problem; 'buggies' are motorized carts, not the pull-carts known as 'trolleys'. Many courses don't have them, or if they do they have only a few to hire. In some cases they are reserved for the elderly or those with health problems. Even if available, their use is often not allowed in winter. There are two reasons for this: first, golf in Northumberland (as it is in Scotland) is for walking and, secondly, the courses may not be designed for carts, which could damage the course in wet conditions. Visitors requiring a cart should check beforehand; don't just assume they will be available.

Caddies

Forget it. Drag it or carry it.

Handicap Certificate

In our years of playing the Northumberland courses we have never been asked for a handicap certificate, even when playing competition. However, it would be prudent to carry a handicap card or certificate, or at least a letter of introduction from your club in which your handicap is stated.

Weather

There are many weather variations across Northumberland on any given day, so if the weather at one course is inclement, another course a short drive away may have playable conditions. Ring around the courses; it's rare not to find somewhere you can play even if the weather is foul where you are. On the rare occasions that Northumberland is closed for golfing business, it's a short hop into Scotland, Tyne and Wear, or Cumbria where the weather may be kinder. We suggest that visitors buy either *The AA Golf Course Guide* or *The Sunday Telegraph Golf Course Guide to Britain and Ireland*. They provide course and contact details for neighbouring counties and Scotland.

As a general guide: the average maximum temperatures in Northumberland range from 7 degrees in January/February to 18 degrees in July/August (four degrees cooler than London). The lowest recorded temperature is minus 12 degrees; the highest 28 degrees. The annual total rainfall is 650mm (26 inches). October and December are the wettest months, April and July the driest. The strongest winds are in January, May and December, but a stiff wind (often cold) is a common occurrence. Snow is more likely in January and February, but the falls are usually light and rarely prolonged.

The coastal strip enjoys on average more sunshine than the rest of Britain, but it can experience *haars* – a Viking word for a dense sea mist formed on sunny days when the cold air above the sea mixes with the warm air above the land. These can seriously affect visibility, but not playing pleasure.

Northumberland's northern position imposes advantages and disadvantages for golfers. Between mid-November to mid-January golf is limited to between 8.30am to 4.00pm, but from mid May to mid July the time for play extends, from 5.00am to 9.30pm. This is no problem because in winter the courses are usually deserted. In summer, many courses have lower green fees if you play after 4.00pm.

Winter Golf

Don't be afraid of playing golf in Northumberland in winter. The weather is cold but typically dry and, as said earlier, even if it rains or snows in one place, you can usually find a course open in others close by. Course closure is rare, and visitors are welcome. The green fees are cheaper and you will often have the course to yourself.

Both men and ladies may have to play from winter tees (synthetic mats a little ahead of the visitors' tees) to smaller (and rougher) winter greens set apart from the real greens. A tip: while the mats accept standard tees it can be a bit of a chore to push them in. Instead, buy a set of winter tees – rubber cones of different heights on which to sit your ball. They are cheap, unbreakable and they also work well on grass.

Equipment

The weather can change quickly in Northumberland, and your dress should allow for unexpected rain and temperature variations during a round. Good wet weather gear is a *must* (we recommend a good quality golf suit that is windproof, waterproof and 'breathable'); you also need a warm hat, preferably one that covers your ears, and warm gloves to wear between shots. A waterproof bag cover will help keep your bag, clubs and kit dry.

Dress in layers: an undershirt of some type, a long-sleeve shirt, a light sweater, and a lightweight over-jacket. If you find you are too warm, room can usually be found in your bag or on your trolley to carry redundant clothing.

Carry plenty of towels to dry your grips and hands, and glasses if you wear them. In cold weather, wearing golf gloves on both hands can help keep them warm, and if wet enhance your grip.

Shoes must be waterproof and a pair of cheap rubber spiked golf shoes (available from larger golf stores) will save your regular shoes in wet and muddy conditions. They will also keep your feet warm.

Course Guides

Many courses have guides on sale through the pro-shops that will assist visitors to understand the course layout and determine hazards and distances from the green. They cost a pound or two, but in addition to making the course more enjoyable they are mementos of the outing.

If your time is limited ...

We are conscious that most visitors are likely to have a limited time in Northumberland, and would need time to see its wonderful scenery and sites as well as play golf. Accordingly, we have suppressed our unease about picking favourites, a highly subjective exercise as evidenced by our preference for links/seaside courses. We believe the courses we have preferred offer the best golfing experience while at the same time locate visitors in country that best represents Northumberland's beautiful scenery and history.

At the top of our list are Bamburgh and Berwick-upon-Tweed (Goswick). The first is a superb seaside course that offers wonderful coastal, countryside and Castle views and challenging golf. Goswick is, in our view, the best of Northumberland's links courses – it's a true links classic as good as you would find in Scotland. We suspect both would rank among the best courses in England. If visitors share our preference for classic links courses, and time allows, Dunstanburgh and Seahouses are highly recommended. They are also fine courses.

Other seaside favourites are Alnmouth (Foxton Hall) and Magdalene Fields. Both have superb views, provide a fair test of golf, and the last brings you into contact with the awesome history of Berwick-upon-Tweed.

Our task was harder in picking parkland courses – there are so many fine such courses in the county. After some debate we have opted for Matfen Hall with its elegant setting and subtle blend of holes. However, the two De Vere Slaley Hall championship courses come a very close second. Hexham and Linden Hall are highly recommended simply because they are interesting, challenging and beautiful courses.

Wooler is our choice for the best moorland course. It's a very physical course and only nine holes (though made a credible 18 holes by creative alternate tee positions), but it's an exceptional golfing experience. The views of the Cheviots and into Scotland from its lofty perch are breathtaking, the golf is challenging, and you can step back into the Iron Age from the 7th hole. Haltwhistle comes in at second place in the moorland category. It's also a physical course but a lot of fun to play. It takes you into Hadrian's Wall country and offers the unique experience of playing golf on a Roman heritage site. Bellingham, with its fine views over the Tyne Valley and moorland and number of great holes, is a third choice for moorland play.

INDEX OF PLACES

*Places with golf courses described in this book are in **bold type***